AMAZING DINOSAURS

DOUGAL DIXON

BOYDS MILLS PRESS

HONESDALE, PENNSYLVANIA

Author Dougal Dixon is an internationally recognized authority on dinosaurs. He is a popular science writer in the United States and Great Britain, and translations of his 140 books have been sold in many other countries. He is the author of more than twenty books about dinosaurs, a number of them for young readers, including *Dougal Dixon's Dinosaurs*. He lives in England.

Scientific Advisor Dr. Peter Dodson is professor of anatomy at the School of Veterinary Medicine and professor of geology at the University of Pennsylvania in Philadelphia. He is also a research associate at the Academy of Natural Sciences in Philadelphia. He has discovered dinosaurs in western Canada, China, Madagascar, Egypt, and the United States. He is also coeditor of *The Dinosauria*, the definitive dinosaur book for scientists.

Copyright © 2000, 2007 by Boyds Mills Press
All rights reserved

Boyds Mills Press, Inc.
815 Church Street
Honesdale, Pennsylvania 18431
Printed in China

Library of Congress Cataloging-in-Publication Data

Dixon, Dougal.
   Dougal Dixon's amazing dinosaurs : the fiercest, the tallest, the toughest, the smallest / Dougal Dixon. — 2nd ed.
      p. cm.
   Includes bibliographical references and index.
   ISBN 978-1-59078-537-9 (hardcover : alk. paper)
   1. Dinosaurs—Juvenile literature. I. Title. II. Title: Amazing dinosaurs.

   QE861.5.D592 2007
   567.9—dc22

                                        2006038922

First edition, *Dougal Dixon's Amazing Dinosaurs*, 2000
Second edition, *Amazing Dinosaurs*, 2007

Book designed and produced by
   Bender Richardson White
   Uxbridge, England

Illustrations by Steve Kirk, Chris Forsey, James Field, Jim Robins, John James.

The text of this book is set in Imago and Joanna.

About This Edition

Dougal Dixon and Dr. Peter Dodson worked together to bring this book fully up-to-date.

First, they added twelve more dinosaurs—many of them new discoveries! In recent years, scientists have found many new kinds of dinosaurs. In addition to the all-time favorites, such as *T. rex* and *Triceratops*, this book includes *Guanlong* (page 31) *Masiakasaurus* (pages 32–33) *Antetonitrus* (pages 40–41) *Melanorosaurus* (pages 40–41) *Brachytrachelopan* (page 45) *Agustinia* (pages 50–51) *Magyarosaurus* (pages 54–55) *Bonitasaura* (pages 56–57) *Achelousaurus* (page 83) *Ouranosaurus* (pages 100–101) *Equijubus* (page 106) *Olorotitan* (page 107).

Second, they worked with expert dinosaur artists to make the illustrations from the first edition match the latest findings. For example, scientists now think that several well-known dinosaurs—such as *Velociraptor* and *Oviraptor*—had feathers. The artists have included their new visions of these dinosaurs, each with a new feathered look.

New findings have also touched this book in many small ways. For instance, the tiny hands of *T. rex* no longer hang down but face each other instead. And *Gastonia* has a full set of spikes on its sides and back.

We hope this completely updated resource will fire young readers' imaginations and help stimulate a lifelong interest in science.

The Publishers

Contents

Dinosaur Family Tree

The word *dinosaur* comes from Latin words and means "terrible lizard." Some dinosaurs were fierce and did look like present-day lizards. But others looked like different kinds of reptiles, such as crocodiles, or they resembled mammals or birds. In fact, birds are the closest living relatives of the dinosaurs.

The idea we all have of dinosaurs is often that of the "terrible lizard," like this *Allosaurus.*

How were dinosaurs related to one another? The meat-eating dinosaurs were all closely related, just as present-day lions, tigers, and house cats are relatives. In turn, the meat-eating dinosaurs were related to the long-necked plant eaters and more distantly related to the two-footed plant eaters and the armored dinosaurs. Page 5 shows the dinosaur family tree.

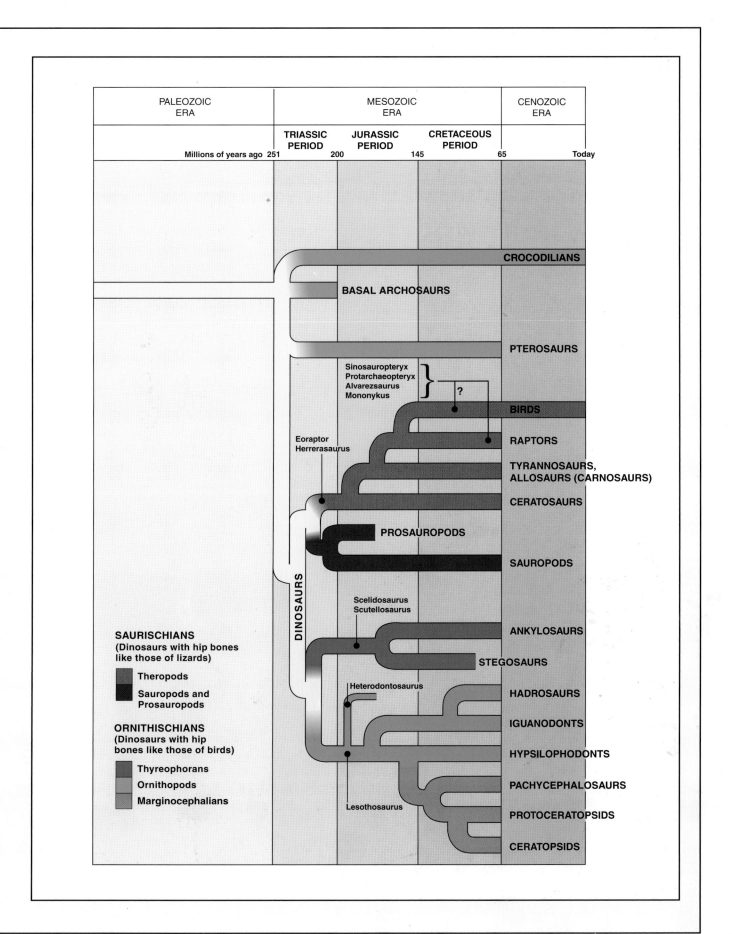

The earliest dinosaurs appeared in South America 228 million years ago. There, they shared the landscape with all kinds of other reptiles. Two of these early dinosaurs were meat eaters. They would have eaten the plant-eating reptiles.

A plant-eating reptile, the size of a modern-day pig, has just been killed by a new kind of animal—the dinosaur *Herrerasaurus*. A larger meat-eating reptile and a small dinosaur, *Eoraptor*, come to take a share of the kill.

KEY
1 *Herrerasaurus*
2 *Eoraptor*

Allosaurus (AL-o-SAW-rus) was one of the biggest and most common of all the meat-eating dinosaurs that lived at the end of the Jurassic Period, around 161 to 145 million years ago. It was built like other meat eaters, with strong legs and jaws.

Powerful neck muscles

Nostril

Eye socket

Small arms

Clawed fingers worked by tendons

Tail helping to balance body

Powerful leg muscles attached to hip bone

Tendons working the toes

Powerful Muscles
Allosaurus ran on its powerful hind legs. Its biggest leg muscles were high up on each thigh. This was ideal for running fast and hunting. *Allosaurus* also had strong neck and jaw muscles.

Strong Claws and Jaws
Allosaurus could curl its fingers like a pincer. It had strong claws to grab and kill its prey. Its long jaws contained rows of sharp teeth for tearing through meat.

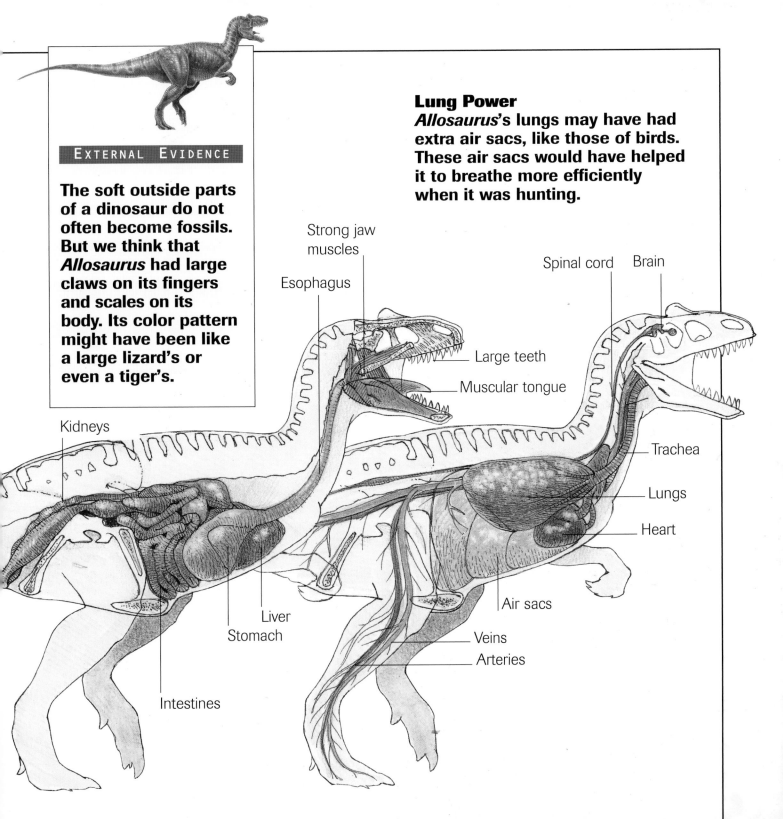

The soft outside parts of a dinosaur do not often become fossils. But we think that *Allosaurus* had large claws on its fingers and scales on its body. Its color pattern might have been like a large lizard's or even a tiger's.

Lung Power

Allosaurus's lungs may have had extra air sacs, like those of birds. These air sacs would have helped it to breathe more efficiently when it was hunting.

Strong jaw muscles

Esophagus

Spinal cord

Brain

Large teeth

Muscular tongue

Kidneys

Trachea

Lungs

Heart

Air sacs

Liver

Stomach

Veins

Arteries

Intestines

Digestive Organs

Allosaurus had short intestines because meat is easier to digest than plant food. (Because plants are harder to digest, plant eaters need bigger stomachs and longer intestines.)

This gave *Allosaurus* a small body compared with plant eaters around at the same time. For this reason, even today's meat eaters, such as tigers and wolves, are usually smaller than plant eaters, such as wildebeests.

9

FACTS AND FIGURES

Herrerasaurus

(huh-RARE-uh-SAW-rus)

Meaning of Name: "Herrera's lizard"—named after its discoverer, Victorino Herrera

Classification: Herrerasaur—a family that evolved before the rest of the meat eaters

Size, Weight: 10–20 feet (3–6 meters) long, 800–1,000 pounds (360–460 kilograms)

Time: Late Triassic, 228 million years ago

Place: Northwestern Argentina

Food: Meat

Eoraptor

(EE-o-RAP-tur)

Meaning of Name: "Dawn thief"—hunted for food at the start of the Age of Dinosaurs

Classification: Basal saurischian from which theropods probably evolved

Size, Weight: 3 feet (1 meter) long, 11–16 pounds (5–7 kilograms)

Time: Late Triassic, 228 million years ago

Place: Northwestern Argentina

Food: Meat, insects

Eoraptor

Eoraptor preyed on other reptiles and may have eaten smaller animals, such as insects. Like modern reptiles, it probably had scaly skin and laid eggs.

Herrerasaurus

Herrerasaurus was a large dinosaur and must have preyed on the big plant-eating reptiles living at the time. It might have swallowed its prey whole, as a present-day snake does. But more probably, *Herrerasaurus* used its strong jaws and sharp teeth to gnaw and bite its food.

Before the dinosaurs existed, there were many other kinds of reptiles living on the Earth. During the Triassic Period, around 251 to 200 million years ago, the first dinosaurs evolved from crocodile-like reptiles. The earliest of these primitive meat-eating dinosaurs have been found in South America. Some were small—about the size of large lizards found today. Others were as big and fierce as tigers.

Pack Hunters

Some meat-eating dinosaurs hunted alone. Others hunted in packs, as wolves do today. A pack of small animals can easily hunt a much larger, slower animal. Together, the animals in a pack can attack a big plant eater from all sides, killing it with many slashes and bites.

Coelophysis
Hundreds of *Coelophysis* skeletons were found in a quarry in New Mexico. All the animals in the pack were gathered around a water hole that had dried up in a drought.

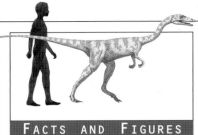
Coelophysis
(SEE-lo-FY-sis)
Meaning of Name: "Hollow form"—because of its hollow bones
Classification: Ceratosaur— a primitive group of meat-eating dinosaurs, some with horns on their noses
Size, Weight: Up to 9 feet (3 meters) long, 40 pounds (18 kilograms)
Time: Late Triassic, 215 million years ago
Place: Southwest United States
Food: Meat, especially smaller reptiles

FACTS AND FIGURES

Syntarsus
(sin-TAR-sus)
Meaning of Name: "Ankle stuck together"—from its foot bones, which were joined
Classification: Ceratosaur
Size, Weight: 10 feet (3 meters) long, 50 pounds (23 kilograms)
Time: Early Jurassic, 199 million years ago
Place: Zimbabwe and Arizona
Food: Meat, probably smaller reptiles

Syntarsus
Syntarsus lived in Africa, while the very similar *Coelophysis* lived in North America. This shows that the two continents of Africa and North America were joined during the Early Jurassic Period and that the same kinds of dinosaurs lived all over the world.

Allosaurus and *Cryolophosaurus* belong to a group of dinosaurs called the carnosaurs. These were the first big meat-eating dinosaurs and existed mostly in the Jurassic Period. The animals had leg bones that suggest that they could not run very fast, and so must have ambushed their prey.

Cryolophosaurus
(CRY-o-LO-fo-SAW-rus)
Meaning of Name: "Frozen crested lizard"—found in the icy Antarctic
Classification: Carnosaur
Size, Weight: 25 feet (8 meters) long, 1,500 pounds (680 kilograms)
Time: Early Jurassic, 200 million years ago

FACTS AND FIGURES

Place: Antarctica
Food: Meat, perhaps other dinosaurs

Allosaurus

Allosaurus hooked its three-clawed hands into the skin of its **prey,** then bit it with its huge mouth to finish the kill. Its teeth had sawlike rear edges to tear through skin and bone.

Allosaurus
(AL-oh-SAW-rus)
Meaning of Name: "Different reptile"—different from other reptiles that had been found
Classification: Allosaur
Size, Weight: 25 feet (8 meters) long, 3,300 pounds (1,500 kilograms)

FACTS AND FIGURES

Time: Late Jurassic, 155 to 145 million years ago
Place: Western North America
Food: Other dinosaurs

In recent years, the remains of huge meat-eating dinosaurs have been found all over the world. We used to think that *Tyrannosaurus* was the biggest and that giant carnivores like this lived only in North America. Now we are finding even bigger meat eaters in South America and in Africa.

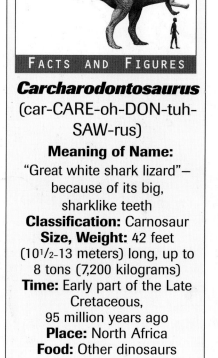

Carcharodontosaurus

We know of only a few bones of this giant, so scientists are unsure if this dinosaur was bigger or smaller than *Tyrannosaurus*. Its skull was 5 feet 3 inches (about 1¹/₂ meters) long, so its mouth was big enough to swallow you or me whole!

Giganotosaurus

In 1995, the skeleton of *Giganotosaurus* was found, and it turned out to be the biggest meat eater known. The closely related and equally big *Mapusaurus,* also from Cretaceous South America, described in 2006, seems to have hunted the big South American plant eaters in packs.

FACTS AND FIGURES

Giganotosaurus
(JIH-ga-NO-toe-SAW-rus)
Meaning of Name: "Gigantic southern lizard"—found in the Southern Hemisphere
Classification: Carnosaur
Size, Weight: 42 feet (13 meters) long, 8 tons (7,200 kilograms)
Time: End of the Early Cretaceous, 112 million years ago
Place: Argentina
Food: Other dinosaurs

FACTS AND FIGURES

Carcharodontosaurus
(car-CARE-oh-DON-tuh-SAW-rus)
Meaning of Name: "Great white shark lizard"—because of its big, sharklike teeth
Classification: Carnosaur
Size, Weight: 42 feet (10¹/₂-13 meters) long, up to 8 tons (7,200 kilograms)
Time: Early part of the Late Cretaceous, 95 million years ago
Place: North Africa
Food: Other dinosaurs

Not all meat-eating dinosaurs hunted and killed big animals. An Early Cretaceous group called the spinosaurs seemed to be well adapted for hunting fish, with long jaws and large claws. They probably waded into rivers and hooked the fish with their claws, just as grizzly bears do today.

Spinosaurs
The whole group of spinosaurs take their name from *Spinosaurus*.

Spinosaurus
Spinosaurus had a narrow, crocodile-like head. It also had a tall fin, or sail, supported by long spines on its back.

Baryonyx

Only one skeleton of *Baryonyx* has ever been discovered. Fish scales and bones were found in its stomach—remains of its last meal.

Suchomimus, a big relative of *Baryonyx,* hunted along African riverbanks 125 million years ago.

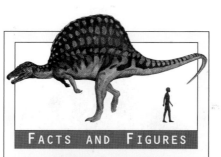

FACTS AND FIGURES

Spinosaurus

(SPY-nuh-SAW-rus)
Meaning of Name: "Spined lizard"—from the spines down its back
Classification: Carnosaur
Size, Weight: 40 feet (12 meters) long, 4–9 tons (3,600–8,000 kilograms)
Time: Beginning of the Late Cretaceous, 95 million years ago
Place: Egypt
Food: Fish

FACTS AND FIGURES

Baryonyx

(BEAR-ee-ON-icks)
Meaning of Name: "Heavy claw"—had a large claw on its thumb
Classification: Carnosaur
Size, Weight: 30 feet (9 meters) long, 3,300–6,600 pounds (1,500–3,000 kilograms)
Time: Early Cretaceous, 130 million years ago
Place: Southern England
Food: Fish

Probably the most fearsome of the hunting dinosaurs were the dromaeosaurs, or "raptors." These were all fast-running animals with long grasping fingers and big claws on their hind feet. They did not kill other animals quickly. Instead, they slashed deep wounds into the sides of their prey and then let it bleed to death.

FACTS AND FIGURES

Velociraptor
(veh-LAW-sih-RAP-tur)
Meaning of Name: "Fast thief"—a quick hunter
Classification: Raptor
Size, Weight: 6 feet (2 meters) long, 30 pounds (14 kilograms)
Time: Late Cretaceous, 83 million years ago
Place: Mongolia and China
Food: Small animals, including dinosaurs

Velociraptor
If you tickle a cat's chest, it holds on to your hand with its front paws and kicks with its hind legs. In 1971, scientists found the skeleton of a *Velociraptor* holding on to the skeleton of a *Protoceratops* in the same way. They had killed each other in a fight.

Utahraptor

Scientists thought that all the dromaeosaurs were quite small until they examined the remains of this huge raptor in 1993.

Utahraptor had big claws on its hands and feet. The longest measured 12 inches (31 centimeters).

Utahraptor
(YOU-tah-RAP-tur)

Meaning of Name: "Thief from Utah"—hunter, so far found only in Utah

Classification: Raptor

Size, Weight: 20 feet (6 meters) long, 2,000 pounds (900 kilograms)

Time: Early Cretaceous, 130 million years ago

Place: Utah

Food: Bigger dinosaurs

Archaeopteryx, discovered about 140 years ago, had a skeleton like that of a dinosaur and feathers and wings like those of a bird. It has always been thought of as the best proof that birds evolved from dinosaurs. Then, in the late 1990s, scientists discovered more proof—fossil animals that were part bird and part dinosaur.

FACTS AND FIGURES

Sinosauropteryx
(SYE-noh-sawr-OP-tair-icks)
Meaning of Name: "Winged lizard from China"
Classification: Uncertain, but somewhere between theropods and birds
Size, Weight: 3 feet (1 meter) long, 9 pounds (5 kilograms)
Time: Early Cretaceous, 125 million years ago
Place: Liaoning Province, China
Food: Insects, small reptiles

Sinosauropteryx
Sinosauropteryx was a small meat-eating dinosaur. Its skin was covered with fine hairlike fibers.

It seems unlikely that any of these animals could fly. Their coverings may have helped to keep them warm, or they may have been used to attract a mate, like the bright tail feathers of a peacock.

Protarchaeopteryx

Protarchaeopteryx was covered in small downy feathers. It also had longer feathers on its arms and a fan of long feathers on its tail.

Protarchaeopteryx
(PROH-tar-kee-OP-tair-icks)
Meaning of Name: "First ancient wing"—an early bird
Classification: Uncertain
Size, Weight: 3 feet (1 meter) long, 9 pounds (4 kilograms)
Time: Early Cretaceous, 125 million years ago
Place: Liaoning Province, China
Food: Insects, small reptiles

Caudipteryx

Caudipteryx had long feathers on its arms and tail. It had few teeth and a birdlike beak.

Caudipteryx
(caw-DIP-tair-icks)
Meaning of Name: "Tail-wing"
Classification: Uncertain
Size: Just over 3 feet (1meter) long, around 12 pounds (5 kilograms)
Time: Early Cretaceous, 125 million years ago
Place: Liaoning Province, China
Food: Insects, small reptiles

Alvarezsaurus
Alvarezsaurus had a flat back, which made its body look more like that of a bird than those of other dinosaurs.

Even today, scientists do not know whether the alvarezsaurs were dinosaurs or birds. They were built like other lightweight meat-eating dinosaurs, but their arms were short and powerful, and they had only one usable claw. Scientists are not sure what these strange arms were used for. Perhaps they were for digging. Or they could be the vestiges of wings. Perhaps the alvarezsaurs were birds that had lost their powers of flight. We do not know whether they had feathers.

FACTS AND FIGURES

Alvarezsaurus
(AL-vuh-rez-SAW-rus)
Meaning of Name: "Lizard of Alvarez"—named after the Argentine historian Gregorio Alvarez
Classification: Uncertain
Size, Weight: 3 feet (1 meter) long, 9–16 pounds (5–7 kilograms)
Time: Late Cretaceous, 89 million years ago
Place: Western Argentina
Food: Small animals

FACTS AND FIGURES

Mononykus
(MAW-no-NY-kus)
Meaning of Name: "Single claw"—because of its one usable claw
Classification: Uncertain
Size, Weight: 30 inches (76 centimeters) long, 9 pounds (4 kilograms)
Time: Late Cretaceous, 83 million years ago
Place: Mongolia
Food: Small animals and insects

Mononykus
Mononykus and its close relative, *Shuvuuia*, were both from Mongolia, while *Alvarezsaurus* and another, *Patagonykus,* were found in South America. This was a very widespread group of specialized dinosaurs.

Toward the end of the Age of Dinosaurs, some of the meat eaters became more and more birdlike. Some big ones, the ornithomimids, looked like ostriches.

Struthiomimus
Struthiomimus was an ornithomimid the size of a present-day ostrich. It may also have been one of the fastest. Some scientists think that it could run as fast as 50 miles (80 kilometers) an hour.

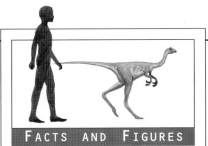

Avimimus
(AH-vee-MIM-mus)
Meaning of Name: "Bird mimic"—thought to look like a bird
Classification: Raptor
Size, Weight: 5 feet (2 meters), 30 pounds (14 kilograms)
Time: Late Cretaceous, 85 million years ago
Place: Mongolia
Food: Unknown

Avimimus
Some scientists think *Avimimus* might have been covered with feathers because its skeleton is so similar to that of a bird. The feathers would not have been used for flying. Instead, they may have helped to keep the animal warm.

Struthiomimus
(STROO-thee-o-MIM-mus)
Meaning of Name: "Ostrich mimic"—thought to look like an ostrich
Classification: Ornithomimid
Size, Weight: 13 feet (4 meters) long, 300 pounds (136 kilograms)
Time: Late Cretaceous, 74 million years ago
Place: Alberta
Food: Small animals, insects, eggs, maybe fruit

Although ornithomimids belonged to the meat-eating theropod group, they may have eaten fruits and tender plants as well as meat. This is similar to the way pandas today are related to the meat-eating cats and dogs.

Troodon

Troodon must have been a good hunter. It had large eyes, keen hearing, and hands that could grasp. It also had agile legs and a long tail, for balance. These would have helped it make quick turns when chasing fast prey.

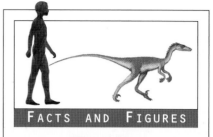

FACTS AND FIGURES

Troodon
(TROH-o-don)
Meaning of Name: "Tearing tooth"—its sharp teeth were the first parts to be found
Classification: Raptor
Size, Weight: 6 feet (2 meters) long, 30 pounds (14 kilograms)
Time: Late Cretaceous, 76 million years ago
Place: Western North America
Food: Meat, particularly small animals

We often think of dinosaurs as being slow, stupid animals. But some dinosaurs, such as *Troodon*, had big brains in proportion to body size. That does not make them very bright compared with humans, but it makes them much brighter than any other reptile we know.

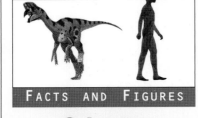

FACTS AND FIGURES

Oviraptor
(O-vih-RAP-tur)
Meaning of Name: "Egg thief"—thought to have been stealing eggs
Classification: Raptor
Size, Weight: 6 feet (2 meters) long, 50–100 pounds (23–45 kilograms)
Time: Late Cretaceous, 83 million years ago
Place: Mongolia
Food: Meat, possibly fruits, insects, shellfish, and grubs

For killing power, *Tyrannosaurus* was unrivaled among dinosaurs. When hunting, it probably hid among the shadows of the forests until its prey approached. Then suddenly it charged. Pushing with its massive legs, it thrust itself forward. It dropped its jaw, opening its mouth and exposing its huge teeth. It swept down its great jaws, tearing off strips of flesh. Its prey died of shock and loss of blood.

Tyrannosaurus
Tyrannosaurus's huge head, strong, sawlike teeth, and little arms make it the best-known and most recognizable of all dinosaurs.

Although *Tyrannosaurus* was one of the biggest of the meat eaters, the earliest tyrannosaurs were quite small animals. *Guanlong* was only the size of a small ostrich.

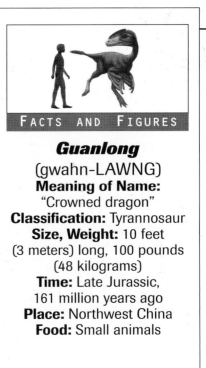

Guanlong
Little *Guanlong* may have been feathered. A baby *Tyrannosaurus* may have had feathers, too.

At the end of the Age of Dinosaurs, some really big and fierce meat eaters roamed the land. In parts of the Northern Hemisphere—in North America and Asia—these were the tyrannosaurs, such as *Tyrannosaurus* itself. In the southern part of the world, they were a group we call the abelisaurs. They were very common in South America and India, but some strange examples also lived on the island of Madagascar. *Masiakasaurus* was one of the smallest meat eaters of Madagascar. It would have eaten any small animal. Its much larger relative, *Majungatholus*, even ate members of its own species— it was a cannibal!

Masiakasaurus
Masiakasaurus was a small abelisaur, not much bigger than a large dog. It probably lived on a diet of fish that it caught in the rivers of the island with its snaggle teeth.

Masiakasaurus
(mah-SHEEK-uh-SAW-rus)
Meaning of Name: "Vicious lizard"—after the local word for "vicious"
Classification: Abelisaur
Size, Weight: 7 feet (2 meters), 80 pounds (35 kilograms)
Time: Late Cretaceous, 84–65 million years ago

FACTS AND FIGURES

Place: Madagascar
Food: Fish

The biggest dinosaurs of all were the long-necked plant eaters, or sauropods. All kinds of sauropods lived together. Some ate from low-growing vegetation. Others had long necks and fed on the leaves at the tops of trees.

Nearly 170 million years ago in central China, herds of plant-eating dinosaurs munch their way through a lush forest by the side of a stream. A pterosaur flies overhead.

KEY
1 *Omeisaurus*
2 *Shunosaurus*

Inside a Giant

The insides of a plant-eating animal are quite different from the insides of a meat eater. Plants are more difficult to digest than meat, so the stomach and intestines of a plant eater need to be large. This means that a plant eater has a bigger body than a meat eater.

Food Requirements
A big sauropod, such as *Seismosaurus*, spent most of its time eating to fuel its massive body. As it digested its food, it also dropped dung. Every day it must have eaten more than 500 pounds (227 kilograms) of food and dropped hundreds of pounds of dung.

Long, whiplike tail

Tail held out, for balance

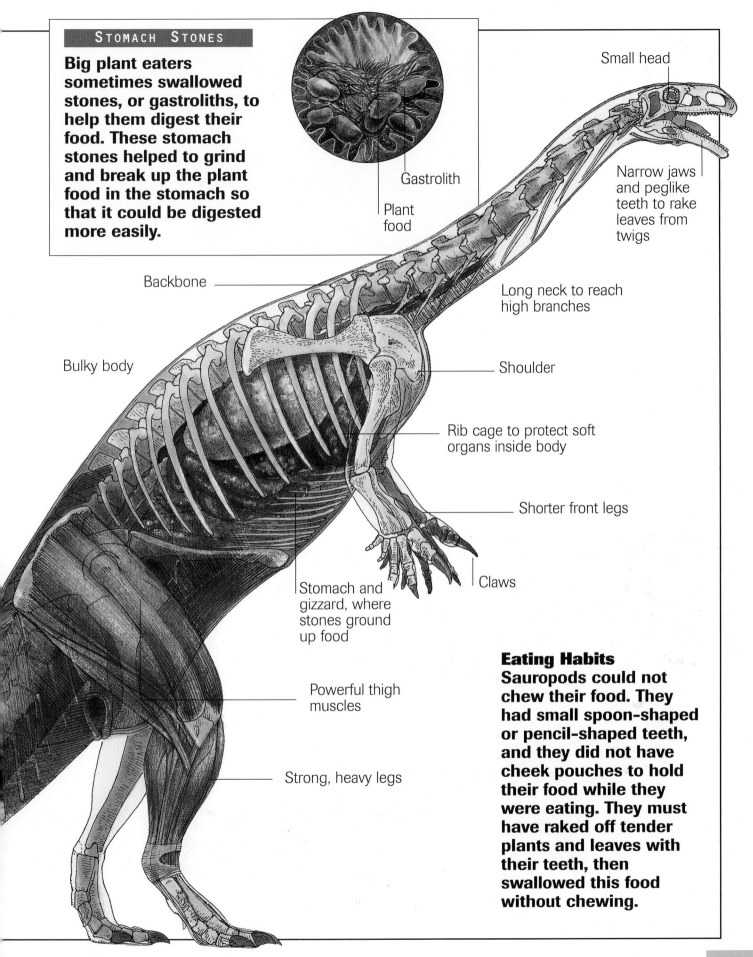

Gastrolith

Plant food

Small head

Narrow jaws and peglike teeth to rake leaves from twigs

Backbone

Long neck to reach high branches

Bulky body

Shoulder

Rib cage to protect soft organs inside body

Shorter front legs

Claws

Stomach and gizzard, where stones ground up food

Powerful thigh muscles

Strong, heavy legs

Eating Habits
Sauropods could not chew their food. They had small spoon-shaped or pencil-shaped teeth, and they did not have cheek pouches to hold their food while they were eating. They must have raked off tender plants and leaves with their teeth, then swallowed this food without chewing.

37

The prosauropods were the first of the really big plant-eating dinosaurs. Like the later sauropods, they each had a small head carried at the end of a long neck. Most of the time they stood on all four legs, but they could rear up on their hind legs for short periods of time.

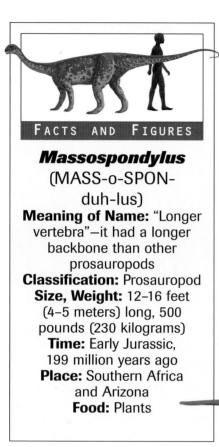

FACTS AND FIGURES

Massospondylus
(MASS-o-SPON-duh-lus)
Meaning of Name: "Longer vertebra"—it had a longer backbone than other prosauropods
Classification: Prosauropod
Size, Weight: 12–16 feet (4–5 meters) long, 500 pounds (230 kilograms)
Time: Early Jurassic, 199 million years ago
Place: Southern Africa and Arizona
Food: Plants

Massospondylus
Massospondylus was a medium-sized prosauropod. It had large eyes and large nostrils, so it must have had good eyesight and a keen sense of smell.

Plateosaurus

(PLAT-ee-o-SAW-rus)

Meaning of Name: "Broad lizard"—had a broad body

Classification: Prosauropod, a group that came before the true sauropods

Size, Weight: 20–26 feet (6–8 meters) long, 1–2 tons (900–1,800 kilograms)

Time: Late Triassic, 216 million years ago

Place: Germany, Greenland, France, and Switzerland

Food: Plants

Flying reptiles called pterosaurs circle around the head and neck of a *Plateosaurus*.

Plateosaurus

Plateosaurus's front feet were built to take its weight, so it must have spent most of the time walking on all fours. However, it may have reared up on its hind legs to fight enemies or to pull down vegetation with its thumb claws.

Bigger and Bigger

In Late Triassic and Early Jurassic times, the big plant eaters were the prosauropods. They could walk on all fours or on just their hind legs. As time went on, some of the prosauropods became bigger and bigger until they looked very like the early sauropods. *Melanorosaurus* was one of these big late prosauropods.

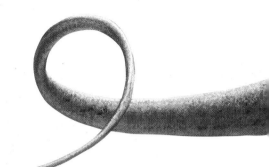

Antetonitrus
Antetonitrus **lived about 15 million years before any other sauropod. The shape of the leg bones and arrangement of the bones of the foot were different in the prosauropods and sauropods. This is how paleontologists tell them apart.**

The early sauropods and late prosauropods actually lived alongside one another at the end of the Triassic. *Antetonitrus* is the earliest-known sauropod.

Melanorosaurus
Melanorosaurus **was a prosauropod. The shape of the leg bones tells us.**

FACTS AND FIGURES

Antetonitrus
(ann-TEE-toh-NIGHT-rus)
Meaning of Name: "Before the thunder"—sometimes the sauropods are called the "brontosaurs," the thunder lizards
Classification: Sauropod
Size, Weight: 26–33 feet (8–10 meters) long, 2 tons (1,800 kilograms)
Time: Late Triassic, 210 million years ago
Place: South Africa
Food: Plants

FACTS AND FIGURES

Melanorosaurus
(meh-LAN-oh-roh-SAW-rus)
Meaning of Name: "Lizard from the Black Mountains"— a reference to the area where it was found
Classification: Prosauropod
Size, Weight: 40 feet (12 meters) long, 3 tons (2,700 kilograms)
Time: Late Triassic, 215 million years ago
Place: South Africa
Food: Plants

A big animal is harder to kill than a small animal. In a place and a time when there were vicious meat eaters, such as *Allosaurus*, a large animal would have been safer than a smaller one. The long-necked plant eaters, or sauropods, would have had little to fear, even from the biggest meat eaters.

FACTS AND FIGURES

Seismosaurus
(SIZE-mo-SAW-rus)
Meaning of Name: "Earthquake lizard"—it was so big!
Classification: Sauropod
Size, Weight: 120–150 feet (37–45 meters) long, 40 tons (36 tonnes)

Time: Late Jurassic, 155 million years ago
Place: New Mexico
Food: Leaves

Seismosaurus
Seismosaurus **was discovered in 1985. Scientists worked out that it was half the length of a football field. The skeleton was firmly buried in hard rock, and it took 10 years to dig it out.**

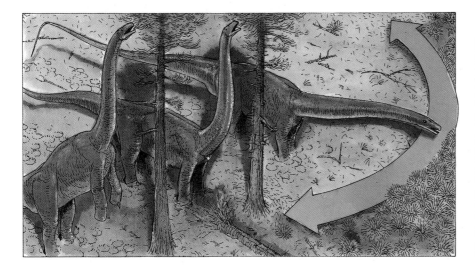

Sweeping Necks
It may have been hard for *Seismosaurus* to keep its giraffelike neck raised for long periods of time. Perhaps it used its neck like the flexible hose on a vacuum cleaner, sweeping its head from side to side along the ground for low-lying vegetation.

Seismosaurus was a giant among sauropods. It probably had to eat during all its waking hours to get the energy it needed. Its legs were shorter than those of its close relative *Diplodocus*. The stumpy legs probably steadied the great length of the animal as it moved.

Producing Dung
As *Seismosaurus* digested its food, it dropped lots of dung. There were probably dung beetles around that broke up the dung, which then fertilized the ground.

Unusual Necks

When *Dicraeosaurus* was discovered in the 1920s, scientists noted that it had spines inside its neck. In the early 1990s, another spiny diplodocid sauropod, *Amargasaurus*, was discovered. These were the first known sauropods with spines.

Dicraeosaurus
Dicraeosaurus had a short neck for a diplodocid sauropod. However, the spines on its backbone would have made it look much bigger and fiercer than it really was. This may have helped to scare away enemies.

FACTS AND FIGURES

Dicraeosaurus
(die-KREE-uh-SAW-rus)
Meaning of Name: "Double-forked lizard"—because of the shape of its backbone
Classification: Sauropod
Size, Weight: 33 feet (10 meters) long, 10 tons (9 tonnes)
Time: Late Jurassic, 155 million years ago
Place: Tanzania
Food: Plants

FACTS AND FIGURES

Amargasaurus
(uh-MAR-guh-SAW-rus)
Meaning of Name: "Lizard from La Amarga"—found in the Amarga canyon in Argentina
Classification: Sauropod
Size, Weight: 33 feet (10 meters) long, 8 tons (7,400 kilograms)
Time: Early Cretaceous, 136 million years ago
Place: Argentina
Food: Plants

Most of the long-necked plant eaters ate tree leaves high above the ground. Brachytrachelopan was an exception. It ate low-growing plants. It had a relatively short neck, and stuck its head into the undergrowth to rip ferns from the ground.

Amargasaurus
When it was first found, scientists thought that the double row of spines on the neck of *Amargasaurus* supported a pair of fins. They do not think so now because the fins would have made the neck difficult to move.

Brachytrachelopan
When scientists found *Brachytrachelopan,* they could not believe how short its neck was. This dinosaur had the shortest neck of any long-necked plant eater and ate plants only from the ground.

Omeisaurus

Datousaurus

Shunosaurus

In the early days of dinosaur hunting, nearly all sauropod skeletons were found in North America. However, during the last 50 years, many long-necks have been found in several regions of China. Their skeletons are well preserved and give us a good picture of what the animals looked like when they were alive.

Shunosaurus
Shunosaurus is the only sauropod we know with a club at the end of its tail. It may have used the club as a weapon, to fight off predators.

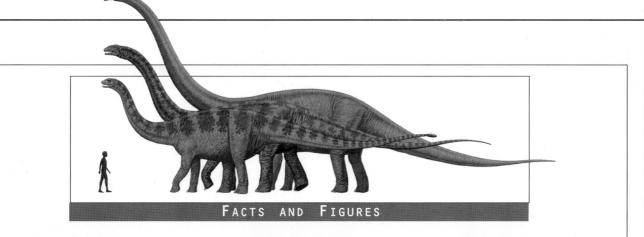

FACTS AND FIGURES

Omeisaurus
(O-mee-SAW-rus)
Meaning of Name: "Sacred mountain lizard"—after a mountain near the spot where it was found
Classification: Sauropod
Size, Weight: 65 feet (20 meters) long, 20 tons (18 tonnes)
Time: Late Jurassic, 155 million years ago
Place: China
Food: Leaves

Datousaurus
(DAT-oo-SAW-rus)
Meaning of Name: "Lizard from Datou"—found in Datou Province, China
Classification: Sauropod
Size, Weight: 50 feet (15 meters) long, 20 tons (18 tonnes)
Time: Middle Jurassic, 165 million years ago
Place: China
Food: Leaves

Shunosaurus
(SHOO-no-SAW-rus)
Meaning of Name: "Lizard from Shou"—the old name for Sichuan Province, China
Classification: Sauropod
Size, Weight: 40 feet (12 meters) long, 10 tons (9 tonnes)
Time: Middle Jurassic, 165 million years ago
Place: China
Food: Leaves

Omeisaurus
Many skeletons of *Omeisaurus* were found in the same place, showing that the animals traveled in herds, as elephants do today.

Datousaurus
This dinosaur was closely related to *Omeisaurus*, which may have been the ancestor of the later diplodocids— the long, low sauropods.

Going for Height

There were many kinds of plants in the Jurassic Period, from low-growing ferns and horsetails to giant conifer trees and tree ferns. It is not surprising, therefore, that plant-eating dinosaurs evolved in different ways to eat these different supplies of food. Some herbivores fed on plants growing close to the ground. Others had long necks and could eat shoots and leaves at the tops of trees.

Brachiosaurus
Brachiosaurus had long front legs that raised its shoulders high above the ground. From these high shoulders, *Brachiosaurus* could stretch its neck into the treetops, as a modern-day giraffe does, and browse on tender shoots.

Different sizes and neck lengths allowed prosauropods and sauropods to eat different sources of food.

KEY

1 *Plateosaurus*
2 *Diplodocus*
3 *Supersaurus*
4 *Brachiosaurus*
5 *Seismosaurus*

Despite their name, the titanosaurs—the last group of sauropods to evolve—were not the biggest dinosaurs. The titanosaur *Agustinia* is noted for its size, but more interesting were the plates that stuck up along the backbone, facing front and back.

FACTS AND FIGURES

Agustinia
(AH-gus-TIN-eh-ah)
Meaning of Name:
"Agustin's one," from Agustin Martinelli, who discovered it
Classification: Sauropod
Size, Weight: 50 feet (15 meters) long, 6-8 tons (5,400–7,200 kilograms)
Time: Early Cretaceous, 125 million years ago
Place: Argentina
Food: Plants

Agustina
Agustina may have had brightly colored skin. Perhaps its spines were brightly colored, too, and were used as signals. Maybe the dinosaur communicated by rattling its spines together to make a noise. Scientists are still uncertain about such things.

At the end of the Cretaceous Period, the two-footed plant eaters had become more common than the sauropods in the northern part of the world. It may be that the two-footed plant eaters fed in the forests of flowering trees while the titanosaurs stayed in the coniferous and fern forests.

The plates on the neck of *Agustinia* were leaf-shaped and in a single row, and those over the back were broader and ended in spines. Paired spines jutted out sideways over the hips, and the spines on the tail were forked. We don't know what these plates and spines were used for, but they were probably for communication of some sort.

The armored skeleton of a *Saltasaurus* was found in 1980. The armor consisted of ridged plates on its back. The discovery showed that all titanosaurs may have had armor. This would have been a useful defense.

Titanosaurs had pencil-shaped teeth like *Diplodocus* rather than the spoon-shaped teeth of *Brachiosaurus*. They must have fed like *Diplodocus*, raking the needles from the conifer trees.

Saltasaurus probably pushed its way through the vegetation, its broad back presenting a solid shield of armor to any attacker.

Saltasaurus
(SAWL-tuh-SAW-rus)
Meaning of Name: "Lizard from Salta"—a place in Argentina
Classification: Sauropod
Size, Weight: 40 feet (12 meters) long, 6–8 tons (5,400–7,200 kilograms)
Time: Late Cretaceous, 83 million years ago
Place: Argentina
Food: Plants

Saltasaurus
The tails of the titanosaurs were flexible, and may have been used as props when the animals were rearing up on their hind legs to reach the treetops.

53

Small-Scale Giant

The long-necked plant-eating sauropods were the biggest land animals that ever lived. Yet *Magyarosaurus* was quite small, with a body no bigger than that of a cow.

At the end of the Cretaceous Period, the landmass of Africa was drifting toward that of Europe. The Tethys Ocean that had existed in between the landmasses was being squeezed out, and the earth movements had thrown up strings of islands off the south coast of Europe. On these islands lived many types of dinosaurs that were like dwarf versions of those we find elsewhere. Small animals evolve because they can make better use of the limited food supply that is found on islands. *Magyarosaurus* was the miniature sauropod of the island chains.

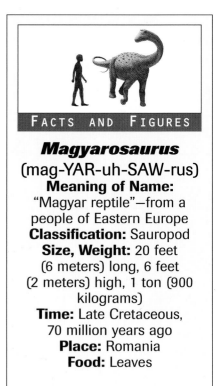

FACTS AND FIGURES

Magyarosaurus
(mag-YAR-uh-SAW-rus)
Meaning of Name:
"Magyar reptile"—from a people of Eastern Europe
Classification: Sauropod
Size, Weight: 20 feet (6 meters) long, 6 feet (2 meters) high, 1 ton (900 kilograms)
Time: Late Cretaceous, 70 million years ago
Place: Romania
Food: Leaves

Magyarosaurus
Except for its size, *Magyarosaurus*
looked like the other armored
sauropods from the end of the
Cretaceous Period.

The body of *Bonitasaura* was very much like that of other titanosaurs, but the head was quite different. It had shearing

Bonitasaura
When scientists first found the skeleton of *Bonitasaura,* they thought that the skull came from a completely different animal because it looked so odd.

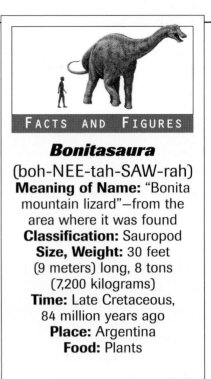

blades at the side of the mouth rather than teeth, and the front of the mouth was straight, like a lawnmower. The mouth must have been used for cropping low plants close to the ground.

By the Cretaceous Period, the main plant eaters in the Southern Hemisphere, where *Bonitasaura* lived, were the sauropods. They evolved into a wide variety of shapes and forms that let them eat all the different kinds of plants that existed there.

Vulnerable in Life

A big sauropod must have been a difficult animal to kill. Its skin was thick, and its head—the most vulnerable point—was far above the ground. However, a group of smaller, meat-eating dromaeosaurs, or raptors, working together like a pack of wolves, could sometimes attack and kill a big plant eater, such as a camarasaur.

Sauropod Versus Raptor
A pack of *Utahraptor* attacking a *Cedarosaurus* in the Cretaceous Period. The raptors would have slashed their prey repeatedly to weaken it, then moved in for the kill.

Argentinosaurus
(AR-jen-TEEN-o-
SAW-rus)
Meaning of Name: "Lizard
from Argentina"
Classification: Sauropod
Size, Weight: 90 feet
(29 meters) long, 40 feet
(12 meters) high, 100 tons
(90 tonnes)
Time: Late Cretaceous,
100 million years ago
Place: Argentina
Food: Leaves

Argentinosaurus
Scientists have found
only a few bones of
Argentinosaurus—but
those bones are huge.
Its lower leg bone is
as tall as a man.

By the end of the Cretaceous Period,
all the continents had split apart and
were slowly moving away from one
another. South America was one big
island continent, just as Australia
is today. And just as koala bears and
kangaroos live only in Australia,
some dinosaurs lived only in South
America. These included the meat
eater *Giganotosaurus* and one of the
biggest animals ever to have lived on
Earth—the plant eater *Argentinosaurus*.

The end of the Cretaceous Period was the time of the fierce carnivore *Tyrannosaurus*. Some plant eaters developed armor of horns, plates, and spikes, which helped protect them from such meat eaters.

Hidden among the trees, *Tyrannosaurus* stalks a herd of duckbills. An armored dinosaur is safe behind its covering of plates.

KEY
1 *Tyrannosaurus*
2 *Edmontosaurus*
3 *Ankylosaurus*

3

By the Late Triassic and Early Jurassic periods, there were many meat-eating dinosaurs around. There were also other meat eaters, such as crocodiles.

Scelidosaurus
Scelidosaurus was the size of a small cow. It had rows of bony knobs running from its skull to the tip of its tail.

Scelidosaurus

(skel-EYE-doh-SAW-rus)

Meaning of Name: "Leg lizard"—early scientists thought its legs were different from those of any other reptile

Classification: Scelidosaur, may be ancestor to the stegosaurs and ankylosaurs

Size, Weight: 13 feet (4 meters) long, 500 pounds (227 kilograms)

Time: Early Jurassic, 195 million years ago

Place: England

Food: Plants

At this time, some of the plant eaters began to develop armor to defend themselves against these hungry predators. The first armor was on the back and consisted of small bony knobs, or shields. If attacked, the armored dinosaur would crouch on the ground so its attacker would get a mouthful of hard, tough bone.

Scutellosaurus

Scutellosaurus must have looked like a knobby lizard with a very long tail. Its back was covered with more than 300 bony studs and spikes.

Scutellosaurus

(skoo-TELL-o-SAW-rus)

Meaning of Name: "Lizard with little shields"

Classification: Uncertain, may be related to both stegosaurs and ankylosaurs

Size, Weight: 4 feet (120 centimeters) long, 20 pounds (9 kilograms)

Time: Early Jurassic, 199 million years ago

Place: Arizona

Food: Plants

The stegosaurs were plate-carrying dinosaurs. Their armor consisted of a double row of pointed plates running along the length of their backs. Most stegosaurs also had a double row of spikes on the end of their tails, which they used as weapons. If in danger, they could swing their tails at their attackers with great force. Some stegosaurs, such as *Kentrosaurus*, also had long spikes sticking out from their shoulders. These helped to protect them if they were attacked from the front or the sides.

Kentrosaurus
Kentrosaurus was the size of a large cow. It had narrow, pointed spikes on its neck and back, and long spikes on its tail.

Huayangosaurus

This is the earliest-known stegosaur found so far. Its front legs were almost the same length as its back legs.

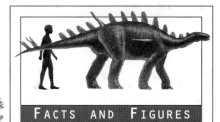

Food for All

The plated dinosaurs were usually smaller than the long-necked plant-eating dinosaurs. They probably ate the lower branches of tall ginkgo trees or plants that grew closer to the ground, such as tough cycads.

Big Plate Carrier

Stegosaurus is probably the best-known stegosaur. It had a spiked tail and rows of wide triangular plates running down its back. Scientists are still not sure what the plates were used for.

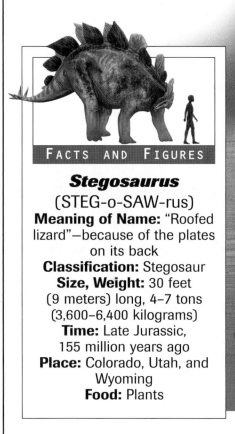

Stegosaurus
(STEG-o-SAW-rus)
Meaning of Name: "Roofed lizard"—because of the plates on its back
Classification: Stegosaur
Size, Weight: 30 feet (9 meters) long, 4–7 tons (3,600–6,400 kilograms)
Time: Late Jurassic, 155 million years ago
Place: Colorado, Utah, and Wyoming
Food: Plants

If attacked, dinosaurs such as *Stegosaurus* and *Huayangosaurus* would turn their backs toward their predators and lash out with their long, spiked tails. Their tails were not powerful enough to kill a big predator, but they might have forced an enemy to look for an easier meal elsewhere.

Stegosaurus
Stegosaurus had a very small head for the size of its body. Like other armored dinosaurs, it had a beak and might have had cheek pouches to help it gather food.

Stegosaurus's plates may have been used as armor. If so, they would have been covered with horn. Perhaps the plates were used to keep the dinosaur cool, rather like the cooling fins of a motorcycle engine. If so, they would have been covered with skin.

The stegosaurs were the main armored dinosaurs of the Jurassic Period, but they died out during the Cretaceous Period. Their place was taken by the ankylosaurs. There were two groups of ankylosaurs— nodosaurids, which had spikes on their backs and sides, and ankylosaurids, which had clubs on their tails.

Minmi
Like a nodosaurid, *Minmi* did not have a club on its tail. But other details in its fossils look like those of an ankylosaurid. Scientists don't agree what to call it!

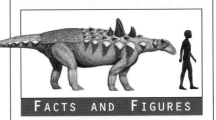

Gastonia
(gas-TOH-nee-uh)
Meaning of Name:
"Gaston's animal"—
after Robert Gaston, who
discovered it
Classification: Nodosaurid
Size, Weight: 20 feet
(6 meters) long, 2 tons
(1,800 kilograms)
Time: Early Cretaceous,
130 million years ago
Place: Utah
Food: Plants

Gastonia
Gastonia had heavy armor of spikes down its back, a mass of tiny shields over its hips, and a double row of plates down its tail. If attacked, *Gastonia* would have been too slow to run away, so it would have crouched to protect its delicate underbelly.

Gastonia defending itself against *Utahraptor*

Minmi
(MIN-mee)
Meaning of Name: "Found at Minmi Crossing"—a place in Australia
Classification: Ankylosaur
Size, Weight: 9 feet (3 meters) long, 500 pounds (227 kilograms)
Time: Early Cretaceous, 125 million years ago
Place: Australia
Food: Plants

Side Spikes

The bigger nodosaurids had huge spikes sticking out of their armored shoulders. These would have scared away many meat eaters. If a nodosaurid were actually attacked, then it would have used its spikes for fighting.

Edmontonia
Edmontonia had spikes that stuck out sideways. The biggest spikes were forked at the end. They may have been used when two male **Edmontonia** were fighting each other for mates or for leadership of the herd—much like bulls locking horns today.

Edmontonia
(ED-mawn-TOH-nee-uh)
Meaning of Name: "From Edmonton"—the capital of Alberta, Canada, where it was found
Classification: Ankylosaur
Size, Weight: 23 feet (7 meters) long, 3 tons (2,700 kilograms)
Time: Late Cretaceous, 70 million years ago
Place: Canada
Food: Plants

Sauropelta
(SAW-ro-PEL-tuh)
Meaning of Name: "Shield lizard"
Classification: Ankylosaur
Size, Weight: 20 feet (6 meters) long, 3 tons (2,700 kilograms)
Time: Early Cretaceous, 112 million years ago
Place: Montana and Wyoming
Food: Plants

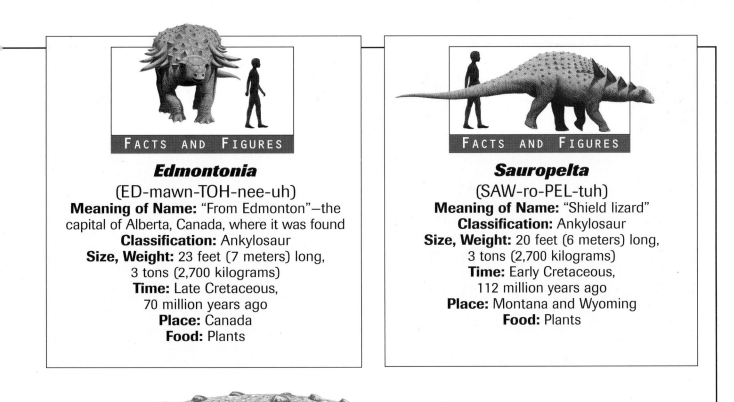

Sauropelta

Sauropelta had shoulder spikes that stuck upward, making the dinosaur look bigger and fiercer than it really was.

The rest of the armor consisted of broad oval plates on the neck and hollow triangular plates on the back and tail.

Sauropelta was the earliest-known of the nodosaurids. It was a common animal living in the Early Cretaceous.

Tail Clubber

Ankylosaurids had a powerful weapon. Each had a massive lump of bone at the end of its tail. The tail bones were shaped to link together so that an ankylosaurid held its tail stiff and straight, like the shaft, or handle, of a club.

The ankylosaurids had strong hip muscles. They could swing their tails to the side with such force that their tail clubs could smash the legs of an attacking meat eater. The ankylosaurids were reptilian tanks!

Ankylosaurus
Ankylosaurus, the most heavily armored dinosaur, was the biggest and the last of the ankylosaurids. Its skull was a box of armored bone. Even its eyelids were armored, slamming shut when danger approached.

Colorful Clubs

We do not know what colors dinosaurs were. Perhaps the meat eaters could see in color. In that case, it would have been useful if a plant eater were camouflaged and could blend into the vegetation. Perhaps plant eaters were a lighter color underneath so that the shadows on the undersides of their bodies would not show up so well.

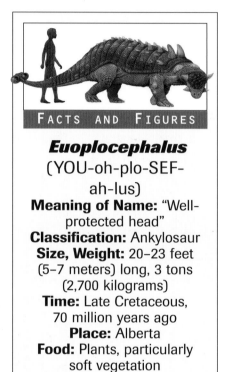

FACTS AND FIGURES

Euoplocephalus
(YOU-oh-plo-SEF-ah-lus)
Meaning of Name: "Well-protected head"
Classification: Ankylosaur
Size, Weight: 20–23 feet (5–7 meters) long, 3 tons (2,700 kilograms)
Time: Late Cretaceous, 70 million years ago
Place: Alberta
Food: Plants, particularly soft vegetation

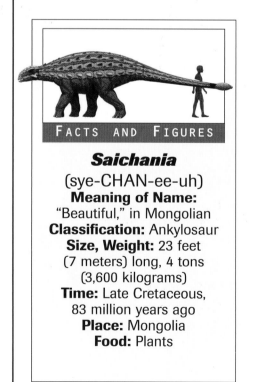

FACTS AND FIGURES

Saichania
(sye-CHAN-ee-uh)
Meaning of Name: "Beautiful," in Mongolian
Classification: Ankylosaur
Size, Weight: 23 feet (7 meters) long, 4 tons (3,600 kilograms)
Time: Late Cretaceous, 83 million years ago
Place: Mongolia
Food: Plants

Some scientists think that the ankylosaurs had bright colors on their tail clubs. If these bright colors were in the shape of a pair of eyes, then an attacking meat eater might attack the club instead of the head—and get a bony mouthful!

Euoplocephalus
Euoplocephalus **is the best-known of the ankylosaurs. Its heavy armor fossilized easily, and a number of skeletons have been found.**

Saichania
This ankylosaur's armor was made up of small studs rather than big plates and spikes. It also had a large nose—probably so that it could smell dangerous meat eaters approaching. A similar dinosaur, *Nodocephalosaurus,* **lived in New Mexico.**

Boneheads

The boneheaded dinosaurs, or pachycephalosaurs, had a solid mass of bone on the top of their heads. They probably used these as battering rams, butting one another's heads to decide who would lead the herd, as mountain sheep do today.

Stygimoloch
As well as a dome of bone, *Stygimoloch* had spiky horns around the top of its head. The scientist who studied it and named it thought that *Stygimoloch* looked like a devil.

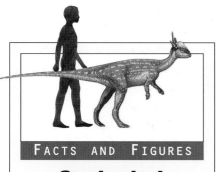

Tylocephale
Scientists only know of part of the skull of *Tylocephale.* However, they can tell what the rest of the dinosaur's head looked like because the skulls of other pachycephalosaurs are well known.

Some scientists think that the boneheads' backbones were very strong, so when two boneheads crashed heads, the shock may not have badly damaged their bodies.

FACTS AND FIGURES

Archaeoceratops
(ARE-kee-o-SAIR-uh-tops)
Meaning of Name: "Ancient horned face"
Classification: Protoceratopsid, a group of small ceratopsians
Size, Weight: 2 feet (70 centimeters) long, 2 pounds (1 kilogram)
Time: Early Cretaceous, 125 million years ago
Place: China
Food: Plants

The ceratopsians were horned dinosaurs. Early ceratopsians, however, were very small and did not have big neck frills or horns like the ceratopsians living at the end of the Age of Dinosaurs. Early ceratopsians could run about on their hind legs or on all fours.

Archaeoceratops
This is a primitive horned dinosaur. Although it did not have horns, it did have the beginnings of a shield around its neck.

Psittacosaurus
(si-TACK-o-SAW-rus)

Meaning of Name: "Parrot lizard"—it had a square head and large beak, like those of a parrot

Classification: Psittacosaur, the most primitive of the ceratopsians, or horned dinosaurs

Size, Weight: 6 feet (2 meters) long, 50 pounds (23 kilograms)

Time: Early Cretaceous, 125 million years ago

Place: Mongolia, China, and Thailand

Food: Plants, perhaps tough stems and fruits

At first, neck frills were simple ridges that helped to hold strong jaw muscles. These muscles gave the animals a powerful bite so they could eat tough seeds and nuts. The ridges slowly evolved into huge armored frills.

Psittacosaurus
Psittacosaurus lived in dry, desertlike areas, where it walked on two legs instead of four. Its large beak was suited for eating tough plants, and the ridge on the back of its skull gave its head a square shape.

The ceratopsids were the big horned dinosaurs. They all looked similar except for the decorations on their heads. Some had one horn. Some had three. Others had several horns growing from the top of their armored neck frills.

Centrosaurus
Centrosaurus had one large horn on its nose. The frill on its head had jagged edges and two hooklike horns.

Centrosaurus
(SEN-tro-SAW-rus)
Meaning of Name: "Sharp-pointed lizard"
Classification: Ceratopsid, the group of big ceratopsians
Size, Weight: 17 feet (5.5 meters) long, 1–2 tons (900–1,800 kilograms)
Time: Late Cretaceous, 74 million years ago
Place: Alberta
Food: Plants

Achelousaurus
(ah-KEE-loh-SAW-rus)
Meaning of Name: "Achelou's lizard"—after a mythical character whose horn was snapped off by Hercules
Classification: Ceratopsid
Size, Weight: 19 feet (6 meters) long, 1–2 tons (900–1,800 kilograms)
Time: Late Cretaceous, 72 million years ago
Place: Montana
Food: Plants

Achelousaurus
The ceratopsids of North America had all kinds of head ornaments. These frills helped them recognize one another and keep to their own herds.

Big Frills

The frills of the ceratopsians were probably used to scare away enemies and to fight them off. The frills may have been brightly colored, with bold patterns and markings. This would have made the dinosaurs look bigger and fiercer than they really were.

Styracosaurus
If attacked, a herd of *Styracosaurus* may have grouped together so that the huge horns of the adults pointed outward, forming a spiky wall.

Albertosaurus

Bigger *Styracosaurus* shielding younger and smaller members of the herd

Horns pointing outward

Styracosaurus

Styracosaurus had a long single horn on its nose and spiky horns around the edge of its neck frill. Its skin may have had bold markings, such as stripes and swirls.

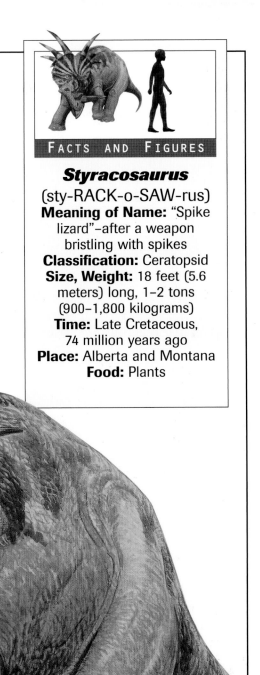

Triceratops
Triceratops was as big as a present-day African bull elephant.

Too Fierce to Attack
The size, sharp horns, and armored neck frill of *Triceratops* would have put off most attackers.

First Fossils
The first fossils of *Triceratops* to be found were its horns. The scientist who studied them thought that they were the horns of some kind of Ice Age bison.

FACTS AND FIGURES

Triceratops
(tri-SAIR-uh-tops)
Meaning of Name: "Three-horned face"
Classification: Ceratopsid
Size, Weight: 25 feet (8 meters) long, 6–7 tons (5,500–6,400 kilograms)
Time: Late Cretaceous, 65 million years ago
Place: Western United States and Canada
Food: Plants

Triceratops had three horns on its head and a large armored neck frill. Many other kinds of dinosaurs had lightly built skulls that fell to pieces before they could be preserved in the rock. However, at 6½ feet (2 meters) long, an armored *Triceratops* skull was so huge that it was often well preserved.

Triceratops is now the most famous horned dinosaur, but it was not the largest. In the 1990s, scientists found even bigger ceratopsid skulls—each 9 feet (about 3 meters) long—belonging to a *Pentaceratops* and a *Torosaurus*.

Big horned dinosaurs, such as Chasmosaurus and Pachyrhinosaurus, were strong and muscular. They needed to be strong to carry the weight of their heavy neck frills and horns and to make long, seasonal journeys in search of new food supplies.

Chasmosaurus
Chasmosaurus had a long skull. Most of this was made up of its neck frill. Holes in the frill helped to make it light. Muscular legs and powerful hips and shoulders helped the dinosaur carry its rhinoceros-sized body.

Digestive Organs
Chasmosaurus had a large stomach and long intestines to help it digest tough plant food.
  Droppings of dung are sometimes preserved as fossils. They tell us what kind of food the dinosaur ate.

Large body

Powerful leg muscles

Thick tail

FACTS AND FIGURES

Chasmosaurus
(KAZ-mo-SAW-rus)
Meaning of Name: "Lizard with openings"—referring to the holes in the neck shield
Classification: Ceratopsid
Size, Weight: 17 feet (5.5 meters) long, 2–3 tons (1,800–2,700 kilograms)
Time: Late Cretaceous, 70 million years ago
Place: Alberta and Texas
Food: Plants

Droppings

The bones of a herd of *Pachyrhinosaurus* were found in Alberta, Canada. The dinosaurs may have drowned in a flash flood as they crossed a river.

We know dinosaurs migrated because we have found vast "bone beds" of dinosaurs. These contain the fossils of many dinosaurs that all died together while they were on the move.

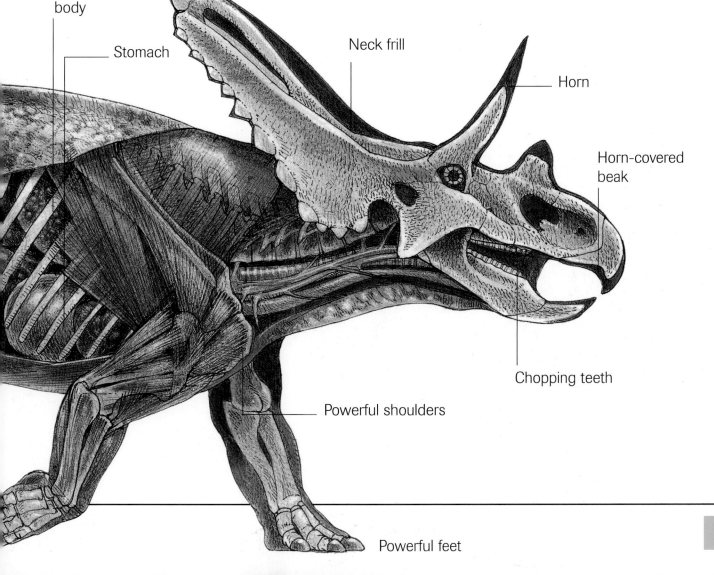

Rib cage to protect soft organs inside body

Stomach

Neck frill

Horn

Horn-covered beak

Chopping teeth

Powerful shoulders

Powerful feet

Two-Footed Plant Eaters

The most common type of plant-eating dinosaurs was a group called the ornithopods. Scientists used to think that all ornithopods walked on two feet. These animals are still called "two-footed plant eaters" even though we now think that the larger kinds spent most of their time on all fours.

Herds of large and small plant-eating ornithopods wade into the shallow water at the mouth of a river to feed on horsetail plants. Nearby, a large meat eater walks away with a fish clasped between its long, narrow jaws.

KEY
1 *Baryonyx*
2 *Iguanodon*
3 *Hypsilophodon*

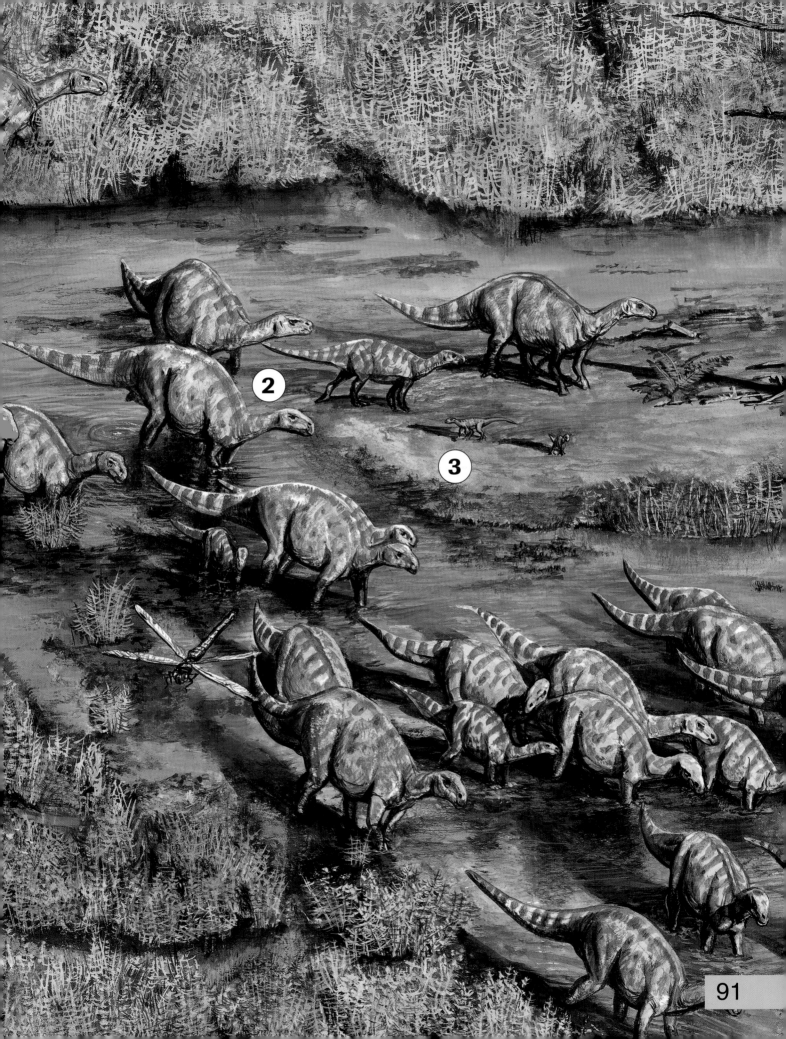

As in other dinosaur groups, the earliest ornithopods were quite small. They must have looked like large lizards running around on their hind legs rather than on all fours.

Heterodontosaurus
Heterodontosaurus had a beak at the front of its mouth and cheek pouches at the side, like all later ornithopods. It was different in that it had sharp fanglike teeth at the front and chewing teeth at the back.

FACTS AND FIGURES

Heterodontosaurus
(HET-ur-o-DON-toh-SAW-rus)
Meaning of Name: "Lizard with different kinds of teeth"
Classification: Heterodontosaur—one of the early ornithopod groups
Size, Weight: 3 feet (1 meter) long, 20 pounds (9 kilograms)
Time: Early Jurassic, 196 million years ago
Place: Southern Africa
Food: Plants, perhaps insects

Lesothosaurus
Nearly all ornithopods had cheek pouches that held their food while they chewed. But *Lesothosaurus*, an early ornithopod, had not developed these.

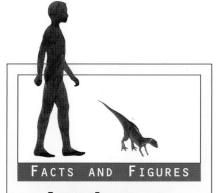

Two-footed plant-eating dinosaurs may have looked like meat eaters, since they both walked on their hind legs. However, plant eaters usually had larger bodies because they needed larger stomachs to digest their food.

Iguana-Tooth

The first remains of *Iguanodon* to be found were bone fragments and teeth. The teeth were very much like those of the modern iguana lizard, which is how *Iguanodon* got its name.

FACTS AND FIGURES

Iguanodon

(ih-GWAN-o-dahn)
Meaning of Name: "Iguana toothed"—teeth like those of an iguana lizard
Classification: Iguanodont
Size, Weight: 33 feet (10 meters) long, 7 tons (6½ tonnes)
Time: Early Cretaceous, 125 million years ago
Place: Western Europe and the western United States
Food: Plants

Iguanodon
Iguanodon had large hind legs, three-toed feet, and shorter front limbs with blunt hooves. It spent most of its time on all fours but may have reared up on its hind legs to pull down branches.

In the 1820s, when *Iguanodon* was discovered, people did not really know what dinosaurs were. Early drawings of *Iguanodon* made it look like a gigantic iguana. It was not until whole skeletons were found in 1878 that people could see its true shape.

Iguanodon Relatives
We know of many close relatives of *Iguanodon*. *Muttaburrasaurus* lived in Australia, *Altirhinus* lived in Asia, and *Ouranosaurus* was found in Africa.

Finger Spikes
Iguanodon's hands had big spikes on the first fingers (what would be our thumbs). It used them to tear down plants. Its little finger was very flexible and would have been used to hold food.

Finger spike

Fast Runners

The hypsilophodonts were the gazelles of the dinosaur world. They had slim bodies and long muscular legs. They would have been able to run away from danger very quickly.

Thescelosaurus
The hypsilophodonts existed until the very end of the Age of Dinosaurs. *Thescelosaurus* was one of the last.

Hypsilophodon

Hypsilophodon was about the size of a modern tree kangaroo, and the scientists who first studied it thought that it may have climbed trees. However, its legs were definitely those of a running animal.

FACTS AND FIGURES

Thescelosaurus
(THES-ke-lo-SAW-rus)
Meaning of Name: "Marvelous lizard"
Classification: Hypsilophodont
Size, Weight: 11 feet (3½ meters) long, 100 pounds (45 kilograms)
Time: Late Cretaceous, 68 million years ago
Place: Western North America
Food: Plants, possibly succulent shoots and buds

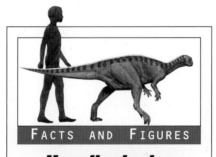

FACTS AND FIGURES

Hypsilophodon
(HIP-sih-LO-fo-dahn)
Meaning of Name: "High-ridged tooth"—from the shape of its teeth
Classification: Hypsilophodont
Size, Weight: 7 feet (2 meters) long, 60 pounds (27 kilograms)
Time: Early Cretaceous, 125 million years ago
Place: Southern England and Spain
Food: Plants

Ornithopod dinosaurs have now been found in Australia, in areas that would have been within the Antarctic Circle during the Early Cretaceous Period. This area was warmer than the Antarctic is today, but these dinosaurs must have been able to survive light frost, snow, and dark days during the Antarctic winter.

Leaellynasaura
The skull of this small dinosaur had big eye sockets. Large eyes must have helped it to see in the dark of the long winters.

Atlascopcosaurus
This dinosaur was named after the corporation that paid for the dig on which its remains were found.

Leaellynasaura
(lay-EL-in-ah-SAW-rah)
Meaning of Name: "Leaellyn's lizard"—after Leaellyn Rich, the daughter of the discoverers, Tom and Patricia Rich
Classification: Hypsilophodont
Size, Weight: 6 feet (2 meters) long, 60 pounds (27 kilograms)
Time: Early Cretaceous, 112 million years ago
Place: Australia
Food: Plants

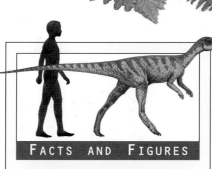

Atlascopcosaurus
(AT-lus-KOP-ko-SAW-rus)
Meaning of Name: "Lizard of the Atlas Copco Corporation," which lent equipment to paleontologists
Classification: Hypsilophodont
Size, Weight: 10 feet (3 meters) long, 100 pounds (45 kilograms)
Time: Early Cretaceous, 112 million years ago
Place: Southeastern Australia
Food: Plants

Cold-Climate Dinosaurs
We usually think of dinosaurs living in hot climates, so scientists were surprised to discover dinosaurs such as *Leaellynasaura*, which had lived in a cold climate.

99

Giant of Africa

While *Iguanodon* lived in Europe, some of its relatives appeared in other parts of the world. *Ouranosaurus* was one that lived in Africa. It had a row of spines down its back, like a picket fence. This may have been covered in skin, or it may have supported a fatty hump—an energy supply when food was scarce.

Ouranosaurus
(ooh-RAN-o–SAW-rus)
Meaning of Name: "Brave
lizard"
Classification: Ornithopod
Size, Weight: 24 feet
(7 meters) long, 4 tons
(3,600 kilograms)
Time: Early Cretaceous,
125 million years ago
Place: Niger
Food: Plants

Ouranosaurus
It is possible that
***Ouranosaurus*'s sail**
was a heat-regulating
device, absorbing
heat from the sun in
the early morning and
giving it off to the
wind in the heat of the
day. In this way, the
sail would have acted
like the sail of
***Spinosaurus*.**

Duckbills

Bactrosaurus
Hadrosaurids lived in North America, Europe, and South America, but *Bactrosaurus*, an early duckbill, lived in Asia.

Toward the end of the Cretaceous Period, one group of ornithopods became the most important plant-eating dinosaurs. These were the hadrosaurs, or the duckbilled dinosaurs. They used their bills to scrape tough needles from conifer trees. Their jaws had hundreds of little teeth for grinding their food.

Duckbill Ancestor
The earliest-known duckbill-like dinosaur in North America—*Eolambia*—lived in Utah in the early part of the Late Cretaceous period. From animals like this, the duckbills evolved and spread over several continents.

Bactrosaurus
(BACK-tro-SAW-rus)

Meaning of Name: "Lizard from Bactria"—a place in Asia

Classification: Hadrosaur—a group of ornithopods with ducklike beaks

Size, Weight: 20 feet (6 meters) long, 1 ton (900 kilograms)

Time: Late Cretaceous, 89 million years ago

Place: China

Food: Plants, especially conifers

Hypacrosaurus
(hye-PACK-ro-SAW-rus)

Meaning of Name: "Almost the highest lizard"

Classification: Hadrosaur

Size, Weight: 30 feet (9 meters) long, 3 tons (2,700 kilograms)

Time: Late Cretaceous, 70 million years ago

Place: Alberta and Montana

Food: Plants, especially conifers

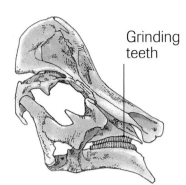

Grinding teeth

Hypacrosaurus

Hypacrosaurus's skull contains forty rows of grinding teeth. These teeth were constantly being worn away and replaced by new ones. This shows that the duckbill ate tough vegetation.

Showy Heads

Parasaurolophus
Parasaurolophus's **crest** consisted of curved and bent tubes. Air passing through this tube would have made a sound like that of a trombone.

Corythosaurus
Corythosaurus got its name from the shape of its rounded crest, which looks like the crest on the helmet of a Corinthian soldier of ancient Greece.

Lambeosaurus
The biggest and most spectacular crests may have been carried only by the males. Perhaps the crests were used mostly to attract a mate.

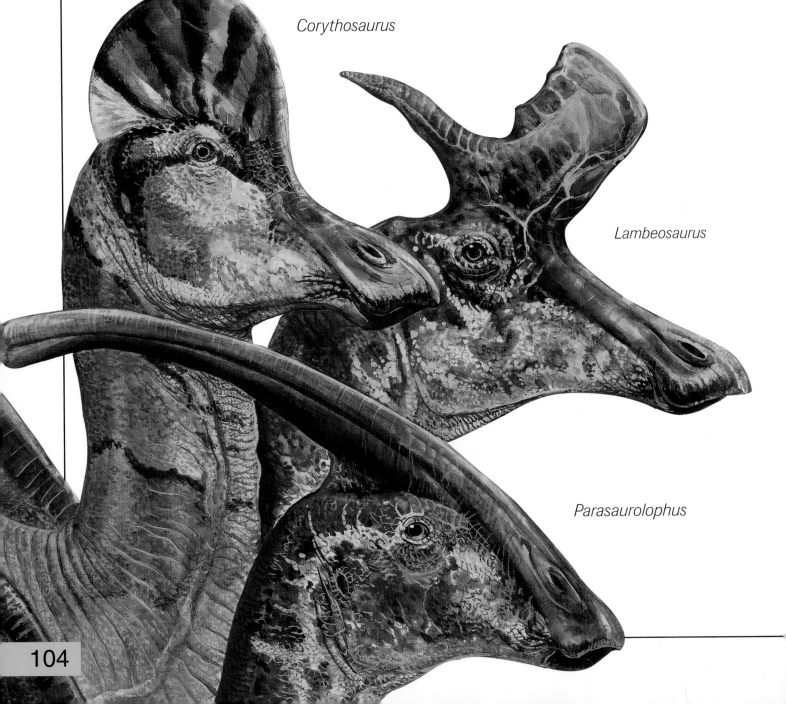

Corythosaurus

Lambeosaurus

Parasaurolophus

Some of the duckbills had large hollow crests on top of their heads. These were probably used to help the dinosaurs recognize one another. They may also have been used for signaling. We do not know whether dinosaurs could make noises, but we think crested dinosaurs communicated by honking or hooting. The sounds they made may have echoed through the forests.

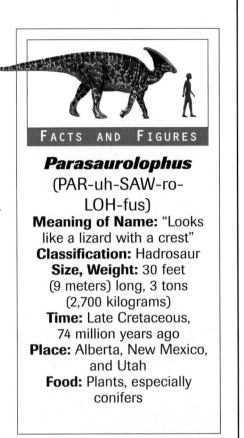

FACTS AND FIGURES

Parasaurolophus
(PAR-uh-SAW-ro-LOH-fus)
Meaning of Name: "Looks like a lizard with a crest"
Classification: Hadrosaur
Size, Weight: 30 feet (9 meters) long, 3 tons (2,700 kilograms)
Time: Late Cretaceous, 74 million years ago
Place: Alberta, New Mexico, and Utah
Food: Plants, especially conifers

FACTS AND FIGURES

Corythosaurus
(kor-ITH-o-SAW-rus)
Meaning of Name: "Lizard with a Corinthian helmet"
Classification: Hadrosaur
Size, Weight: 30 feet (9 meters) long, 3 tons (2,700 kilograms)
Time: Late Cretaceous, 74 million years ago
Place: Alberta
Food: Plants, especially conifers

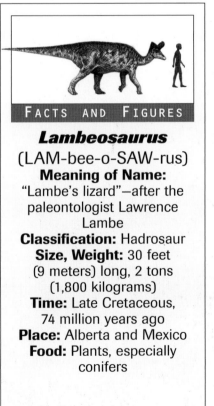

FACTS AND FIGURES

Lambeosaurus
(LAM-bee-o-SAW-rus)
Meaning of Name: "Lambe's lizard"—after the paleontologist Lawrence Lambe
Classification: Hadrosaur
Size, Weight: 30 feet (9 meters) long, 2 tons (1,800 kilograms)
Time: Late Cretaceous, 74 million years ago
Place: Alberta and Mexico
Food: Plants, especially conifers

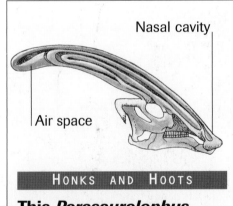

Nasal cavity

Air space

HONKS AND HOOTS

This *Parasaurolophus* skull shows hollow channels running from the nose bones through the crest. Air from the nostrils had to pass through the channels before reaching the lungs. This may have allowed the dinosaur to honk or hoot loudly.

It seems there were more types of duck-billed dinosaurs than any other kind. New ones are being discovered all the time.

One important new duckbill is *Equijubus*, found in 2003. It is the earliest duckbill known, and its skull is similar to that of *Iguanodon*. But it has the large number of grinding teeth and the chewing mechanism of a duckbill.

FACTS AND FIGURES

Equijubus
(ECK-wee-JOOB-us)
Meaning of Name: "Horse's mane"—the local name of the mountain range where it was found
Classification: Hadrosaur-like
Size, Weight: 12 feet (3.5 meters) long, 150 pounds (70 kilograms)
Time: Early Cretaceous, 112 million years ago
Place: Northwest China
Food: Tough plants

Equijubus
The *Iguanodon* shape to the skull, and the hadrosaur-like arrangement of teeth, show that *Equijubus* was a link between the two dinosaur groups.

Olorotitan
(OH-lo-roh-TIGHT-un)

Meaning of Name: "Giant swan"
Classification: Hadrosaur
Size, Weight: 30 feet (9 meters), 3 tons (2,700 kilograms)
Time: Late Cretaceous, 70 million years ago
Place: Eastern Russia
Food: Plants, especially conifers

These clues from *Equijubus* show that the duckbills evolved from *Iguanodon*, or one of its relatives in Asia, and then spread over the whole of the Northern Hemisphere. A much later duckbill, also described in 2003, is *Olorotitan*—one of those with a big crest.

Olorotitan
The crest of this duckbill swept back from the top of the skull and broadened into an upright blade. As with all the other crested duckbills, the crest would have been used for signaling to other dinosaurs.

Nests and Eggs

Scientists know about the lifestyle of some dinosaurs because they have found fossilized nests containing eggs and youngsters. Some ornithopods, such as *Hypacrosaurus*, lived in herds. Many females made nests together, in the same area, for protection.

Nesting Colony
A *Hypacrosaurus* nesting colony was found at Devil's Coulee in Alberta. The nests were spaced apart so that there was room for each mother to walk around, and sit on, her nest without damaging the others.

Hypacrosaurus Nests
Each *Hypacrosaurus* nest was a mound of soil with a shallow hole scooped out of the top. Eggs were laid in the nest in a spiral pattern and may have been covered with vegetation to keep them warm. The hatchlings probably left the nest as soon as they hatched.

Hatching Dinosaur
A dinosaur egg was like that of a modern bird. The baby grew inside, feeding on the yolk. A protective membrane and a tough shell protected the growing baby.

Some baby dinosaurs may have had a little horn on their noses, just as birds do. These would have helped them break out of the shell. The horns may have fallen off after a few days.

Dinosaur eggs came in many sizes. The biggest were about the size of a soccer ball. Bigger eggs had to have thicker shells to hold their contents without cracking. If an egg were too big, a baby dinosaur would not be able to break the egg's thick shell.

Safety in Speed

There were many fast-footed meat-eating dinosaurs during the Age of Dinosaurs. Many of the smaller ornithopod dinosaurs evolved into fast runners. They could escape from the larger meat eaters.

Elaphrosaurus
Elaphrosaurus was typical of the fast-running meat eaters that hunted the two-footed plant eaters. It hunted the hypsilophodont *Dryosaurus* in Late Jurassic Africa. Similarly, fleet-footed *Troodon* hunted the nimble *Orodromeus* in Late Cretaceous Montana.

KEY
1 *Elaphrosaurus*
2 *Dryosaurus*

The legs of a running animal—meat eater or plant eater—have short thigh bones to which all the muscles are attached. The rest of the legs and the feet are long and slender, making them light and easy to move quickly.

We can tell that fast-running meat-eating dinosaurs sometimes caught up with fast-running plant eaters. At nesting sites of fast-running *Troodon* we find the half-eaten remains of the swift *Orodromeus* that had been caught, killed, and brought back to the nest to feed the *Troodon* young.

Dryosaurus
Dryosaurus—like the hypsilophodonts—had legs that were built for speed. It could often outrun its predators.

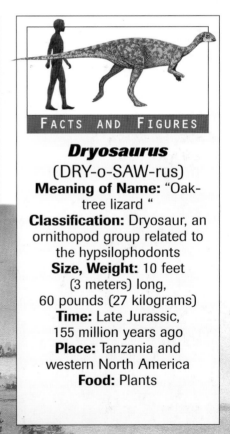

FACTS AND FIGURES

Elaphrosaurus
(ih-LAH-fro-SAW-rus)
Meaning of Name: "Lightweight lizard"
Classification: Ceratosaur, like Syntarsus, page 13
Size, Weight: 17 feet (5 meters) long, 400 pounds (180 kilograms)
Time: Late Jurassic, 155 million years ago
Place: Tanzania
Food: Meat

FACTS AND FIGURES

Dryosaurus
(DRY-o-SAW-rus)
Meaning of Name: "Oak-tree lizard "
Classification: Dryosaur, an ornithopod group related to the hypsilophodonts
Size, Weight: 10 feet (3 meters) long, 60 pounds (27 kilograms)
Time: Late Jurassic, 155 million years ago
Place: Tanzania and western North America
Food: Plants

The biggest meat-eating dinosaurs ate big plant eaters. At the end of the Cretaceous Period, the duckbills were among the larger plant eaters, and one of the biggest duckbills was *Edmontosaurus*. *Edmontosaurus* lived in herds. If a large meat eater, such as a tyrannosaur, killed one of them, the rest of the herd would be safe for a few days while the meat eater consumed its huge feast.

Meat-Eating Enemy
Edmontosaurus could easily be killed by *Tyrannosaurus*. The meat eater's powerful teeth and strong jaws would have torn into the flesh of a cornered *Edmontosaurus*, giving it no means of escape.

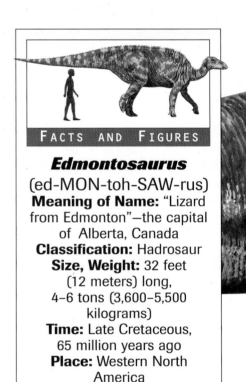

FACTS AND FIGURES

Edmontosaurus
(ed-MON-toh-SAW-rus)
Meaning of Name: "Lizard from Edmonton"—the capital of Alberta, Canada
Classification: Hadrosaur
Size, Weight: 32 feet (12 meters) long, 4–6 tons (3,600–5,500 kilograms)
Time: Late Cretaceous, 65 million years ago
Place: Western North America
Food: Plants, especially conifers

SCAVENGER OR PREDATOR?

Some scientists think that the biggest meat eaters, such as *Tyrannosaurus*, chased and killed their own prey. Others think that they were scavengers, eating animals that had already been killed. Perhaps they were both. In any case, their prey would have been the plant-eating dinosaurs living at the time.

Edmontosaurus

Edmontosaurus was one of the biggest, last, and best-known of the hadrosaurs of North America. We know it from the many complete skeletons that have been found. We have even found preserved impressions of its skin, which are very rare for any dinosaur.

Tyrannosaurus attacking an *Edmontosaurus*

Death and Decay

When an animal dies on land, its body is usually eaten by other animals, and the parts that cannot be eaten rot away. That is why we do not often find the whole preserved remains of dinosaurs.

Dinosaurs to Rocks
A herd of *Iguanodon* drown, and their bodies are washed down a river from the surrounding hills. The bodies of other dead animals are eaten by predators, but the *Iguanodon* bones, lying in a dip in the ground, are not disturbed. The bones eventually turn to fossils and remain hidden for millions of years.

1 An *Iguanodon* dies by a muddy stream or drowns in a flash flood.

2 The meat and the other soft body parts rot away, leaving only the bones of the skeleton. The skeleton starts to get buried by mud and sand washed down by the stream.

3 The skeleton is buried under layers of sediment. Forces and pressure deep inside Earth turn these layers into beds of rock, and the bones are filled with minerals.

4 The fossil skeleton lies hidden in rocks below our feet.

However, if a dinosaur fell into a river or lake and its body were quickly covered by mud and sand, other animals could not eat it. Then it would decay and become fossilized.

Discovery

Dinosaur fossils may remain buried in rock for millions of years. Sometimes, the rock above is worn away, and the fossils become exposed. Then they can be collected and studied by paleontologists, who try to find out about the life of the past.

Paleontologists
Paleontologists study maps to look for promising sites of dinosaur remains. Then, they may set out on scientific expeditions to try to find them.

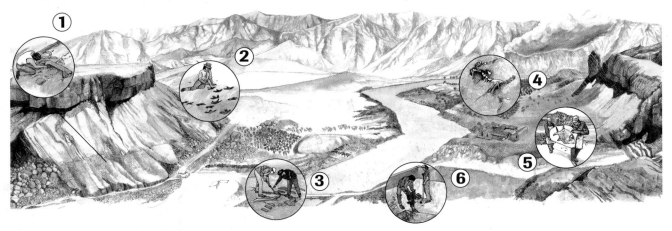

How Fossils Are Found

1 Some dinosaur skeletons are found by scientists. They know where to look because they have studied the types and ages of rocks in which they are likely to find dinosaur fossils.

2 Dry desert winds sometimes wear away rock, uncovering fossils.

3 Some fossils are washed out by rivers, which wear away the rocks.

4 If a fossil has been exposed naturally, by the wind or the rain, it is often found accidentally by people passing by.

5 and 6 When a new find is reported, paleontologists come and study the remains. They may cut the fossils out of the rock and take them back to a laboratory.

Examining Fossil Finds

1 Digging Up the Bones

Wherever a fossil shows in the rock, paleontologists carefully expose more of the bone. They may find many bones, one by one or jumbled together. The scientists dig around the fossils to remove the sections of rock that hold them. Then the team wraps each section in strips of bandage soaked in plaster of Paris. The plaster hardens to form a protective case around the fossil.

2 Uncovering the Bones

At the museum, the protective cases are cut open. Then, skilled technicians called preparators use delicate tools to free each fossil from any remaining rock in which it is buried.

3 The Final Step

Separating the bones from the rock can take months, especially if the technicians have to use acid to eat away at the rock around the bones. Finally, the scientists can study the fossils and find out a little more about the dinosaurs.

Do You Know?

When did the dinosaurs first appear?
The earliest dinosaurs we now know are called *Eoraptor* and *Herrerasaurus*. These meat eaters lived in South America at the start of the Late Triassic Period. They evolved from crocodile-like animals about 228 million years ago.

When did the dinosaurs die out?
Dinosaurs became extinct at the very end of the Cretaceous Period, about 65 million years ago.

How are dinosaurs named?
A dinosaur's proper scientific name (in fact, the proper scientific name for all animals) consists of two parts. The first part, the genus, has a capital letter. The second part, the species, does not. Both are written in italics or underlined. The first scientist to describe a new type of dinosaur usually chooses its name. The name is often taken from a person, a place, or a particular feature of the dinosaur.

Psittacosaurus

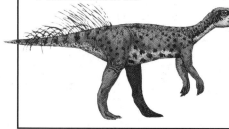

How many kinds of dinosaurs are there?
Scientists know of more than 500 different genera of dinosaurs (genera is the plural of genus). This figure is probably just a quarter of all dinosaur genera that existed.

Which area had the most kinds of dinosaurs?
Most different kinds of dinosaurs are known from three main areas: the United States and Canada, Argentina in South America, and China and Mongolia.

Which were the most wide-ranging dinosaurs?
Iguanodon, from the United States and various parts of Europe, was likely to have been one of the most widespread. Other wide-ranging dinosaurs included *Brachiosaurus*, from Colorado and Tanzania; *Pachyrhinosaurus*, from Alberta and Alaska; *Psittacosaurus*, from China and Mongolia; and *Chasmosaurus*, from Texas and Alberta.

Which was the tallest dinosaur?
Sauroposeidon, a big relative of *Brachiosaurus*, could have raised its head 60 feet (18 meters) above the ground.

Which was the heaviest dinosaur?
As far as we know, *Argentinosaurus* was the heaviest. In life, it would have weighed 100 tons (90 tonnes).

Which was the longest dinosaur?
Seismosaurus, meaning "earthquake lizard," was a sauropod, like *Diplodocus*. From the incomplete skeleton discovered in 1985, scientists think that the whole animal must have been 120–150 feet (37–45 meters) long.

Which was the most heavily armored dinosaur?
The **ankylosaurs**, such as *Euoplocephalus*, are regarded as the most heavily armored dinosaurs—they even had armored eyelids. The biggest, *Ankylosaurus*, was about 25 feet (8 meters) long. *Saichania* from Mongolia had armor on its belly as well as on its back.

Euoplocephalus

Which dinosaur had the biggest skull?

The ceratopsians, or horned dinosaurs with big frills covering their necks, had the biggest skulls. Some specimens of *Torosaurus* and *Pentaceratops* had skulls 9 feet (nearly 3 meters) long—the longest known of any land animal ever.

Which was the smallest dinosaur?

Microraptor, a tree-living, gliding dinosaur from China, was only 2½ feet (77 centimeters) long.

Which dinosaur had the longest neck?

A complete skeleton of *Mamenchisaurus*, a *Diplodocus*-like sauropod from China, has a neck that is 36 feet (11 meters) long, the longest known of any animal.

Which dinosaur had the longest horns?

The three-horned dinosaur, *Triceratops*, had a horn on its nose and one over each eye. The bony cores of the eye horns were more than 3 feet (1 meter) long. They must have been much longer in life, when they would have had a covering of horn.

Which dinosaur had the longest crest?

Parasaurolophus, one of the duckbilled dinosaurs, had a hollow crest that swept back from the skull a distance of 5 feet (about 1½ meters).

Which was the most intelligent dinosaur?

Troodon, a small meat eater from Late Cretaceous Canada, may have been the most intelligent dinosaur. Its brain size, compared to the size of its body, was about the same as that of some modern birds.

Which dinosaur had the biggest sail?

Spinosaurus was a meat eater that may have been as big as *Tyrannosaurus*. On its back, it carried a crest that was supported by 5-foot-long (1½-meter-long) spines from its backbone.

Troodon

Which was the fastest dinosaur?

A little, unknown dinosaur living in Arizona in the Early Jurassic Period left intriguing footprints in the rocks. The animal weighed about 20 pounds (9 kilograms), yet it made footprints that were about 12 feet (3½ meters) apart. The animal must have been running at 40 miles (64 kilometers) an hour.

Which dinosaur had the biggest teeth?

The meat eater *Giganotosaurus* had teeth that were almost 12 inches (30 centimeters) long including the root that was embedded in the jawbone. The exposed part of the teeth was about 6 inches (15 centimeters) long.

Which were the longest-lived dinosaurs?

We cannot tell how long each dinosaur lived, but we think that the long-necked plant eaters lived longer than the others. If they were warm-blooded, they may have lived to an age of 60 years. If they were cold-blooded, they may have survived for about 200 years.

Which museum has the most types of dinosaur?

The American Museum of Natural History in New York City has the most, with at least 100 different species.

Glossary

ankylosaur Armored dinosaur, such as *Euoplocephalus*, covered with bony spikes, knobs, and plates.

beak A horn-covered mouth structure with no teeth that occurs on birds and some dinosaurs. It is lighter than a set of teeth, and is used to gather food.

browse To feed on shoots, leaves, and bark of shrubs and trees.

camouflaged Having a natural color scheme or pattern that allows an animal to blend in with its surroundings so that it will not be noticed.

carnivore A meat-eating animal.

ceratopsian Horned dinosaur, such as *Triceratops*, with a sheet of bone, called a frill or shield, growing from the back of its skull.

cheek pouch A fold of skin and muscle at the side of an animal's mouth that holds its food while it chews.

climate The average weather conditions in a particular part of the world.

cold-blooded Term used to describe an animal, such as a fish or a reptile, whose temperature changes from day to night and which needs less food than a warm-blooded animal.

conifer tree A tree that produces seeds in cones—for example, pine, fir, and larch. The needle-like leaves usually stay on the tree all year.

continent A huge area of land on Earth. The modern continents are (from largest to smallest): Asia, Africa, North America, South America, Antarctica, Europe, and Australia.

crest A structure on top of the head, usually for display.

Cretaceous The final period of geological time between 145 and 65 million years ago. It was at the end of the Age of Dinosaurs.

cycad A plant related to the conifers consisting of a stout trunk and palm-like leaves.

digest To break down food in the stomach and intestines so that it can be absorbed by the body.

evolved Changed, over many generations, to produce new species.

fang A long, pointed tooth.

fern A plant that makes no flowers, with finely divided leaves known as fronds.

flash flood A sudden rush of water down a river valley following rainfall in nearby mountains or high ground.

fossilized Turned into fossils.

fossil Part or trace of once-living plant or animal that is preserved in rocks.

ginkgo Tree that looks like a conifer but with broad leaves that are shed in the fall. There is only one living species, the maidenhair tree.

graze To eat low-growing plants. Sheep, cattle, and other modern grazers eat grass. But there was no grass in dinosaur times.

hatchling An animal that is newly hatched from its egg.

herbivore A plant-eating animal.

hoof A very tough and heavy toenail built to take the weight of an animal.

horn Tough, shiny substance made of the same chemical material as hair and fingernails, and often formed as a protective covering on some part of an animal. The name is also used for a pointed structure covered with horn.

horsetail A simple non-branching plant related to ferns, with segmented (or jointed) stems and tiny leaves.

impression A mark or print in the surface of the ground or a rock made by something pressing against or in it.

intestines The parts of the food canal below the stomach from which nutrients are absorbed into the blood for use by the cells and tissues of the body.

Jurassic The period of geological time between 200 and 145 million years ago. It was the middle period of the Age of Dinosaurs.

mammal A vertebrate (backboned) animal that produces live young and feeds them milk. Modern mammals include cats, dogs, mice, rabbits, whales, monkeys, and humans.

migrate To move from place to place as conditions change to find new sources of food or shelter or to mate and bring up young.

mineral A substance formed naturally in the ground. Minerals are formed from elements such as iron, aluminum, potassium, carbon, silicon, oxygen, and hydrogen. All rocks are made up of minerals.

Ornitholestes grabs a young crocodile from its nest. *Ornitholestes* probably swallowed its prey whole.

ornithopod A two-footed plant-eating dinosaur, such as *Iguanodon*.

paleontologist A person who studies paleontology, the science of fossil life from early times.

plaster of Paris A mixture of fine powder (containing the mineral gypsum) and water that sets hard. Doctors use it to set broken bones, and paleontologists use it to protect delicate fossils as they are moved from the field to the laboratory.

predator A meat-eating animal that hunts and kills other animals for food.

prey An animal that is hunted and eaten by a predator.

pterosaur A flying reptile related to the dinosaurs. Pterosaurs flew using wings of skin stretched from the body to a single, long finger bone.

reptile A cold-blooded vertebrate (backboned) animal that reproduces by laying hard-shelled or leathery eggs on land. Modern-day reptiles include snakes, lizards, turtles, and crocodiles.

sauropod A long-necked plant-eating dinosaur, such as *Brachiosaurus*, that walked on all fours.

scale In reptiles, a small leaf of horn that forms part of the outer covering of the body.

scavenger An animal that eats the bodies of animals that are already dead.

sediment Pieces of soil and rock carried by wind or water and deposited on the bottom of rivers, lakes, and streams.

species A group of living things in which individuals look like one another and, in higher animals, breed with one another to produce young. *Breeding, mating,* and *reproduction* are all terms to describe the process by which individuals make more of their species.

stegosaur An armored dinosaur carrying a double row of pointed plates along its back. *Stegosaurus* is the best-known stegosaur.

tendon A tough piece of animal tissue that attaches muscle to bone.

theropod A meat-eating dinosaur, such as *Tyrannosaurus*.

tree fern A plant of the fern family that grows to 80 feet (24½ meters) or more in height. There are only a few living species, but they were plentiful at the beginning of the Age of Dinosaurs.

Triassic The period of geological time between 251 and 200 million years ago. The dinosaurs first appeared in the Triassic Period.

vegetation Plant life.

vestige A reduced structure or organ representing something that was once useful and developed.

warm-blooded Term used to describe an animal whose body temperature does not change from night to day and which needs large amounts of food.

Dilophosaurus attacks a small *Syntarsus*, another crested meat-eating dinosaur.

Index

Suggested Reading

Barnum Brown: Dinosaur Hunter by David Sheldon. Walker Books for Young Readers, 2006.

Digging for Bird-Dinosaurs: An Expedition to Madagascar by Nic Bishop. Houghton Mifflin, 2002.

Dinosaur Atlas by DK Publishing. DK Children, 2006.

A Dinosaur Named Sue: The Find of the Century by Fay Robinson with the SUE Science Team of The Field Museum. Cartwheel, 1999.

Dinosaurs: A Natural History by Paul Barrett, illustrated by Raul Martin. Simon & Schuster, 2002.

Dinosaur Worlds by Don Lessem. Boyds Mills Press, 1996.

Dougal Dixon's Dinosaurs, Third Edition by Dougal Dixon. Boyds Mills Press, 2007.

Encyclopedia Prehistorica Dinosaurs: The Definitive Pop-Up by Robert Sabuda, illustrated by Matthew Reinhart. Candlewick, 2005.

Feathered Dinosaurs of China by Gregory C. Wenzel. Charlesbridge Publishing, 2004.

The Field Mouse and the Dinosaur Named Sue by Jan Wahl, illustrated by Bob Doucet. Cartwheel, 2000.

The Fossil Feud: Marsh and Cope's Bone Wars by Meish Goldish. Bearport Publishing, 2006.

The Illustrated Encyclopedia of Dinosaurs by Dougal Dixon. Lorenz Books, 2006.

Tyrannosaurus, one of the last of the dinosaurs.